You Don't Have to be a Bag Lady!
A Humorous Survival Guide for the Reluctant Investor

By

Sheila Peters

© 2001, 2002 by Sheila Peters. All rights reserved.

No part of this book may be reproduced, stored in a retrieval system, or transmitted by any means, electronic, mechanical, photocopying, recording, or otherwise, without written permission from the author.

ISBN: 0-7596-8718-8

This book is printed on acid free paper.

1stBooks - rev. 04/18/02

To Mal

Acknowledgments

Cover design by Patricia Andrew
Illustration by Dan Blascoe

Table Of Contents

Introduction The Invisible Fence ix

Chapter 1   Money and Women 1

Chapter 2   Money & Love 11

Chapter 3   Money & Power 19

Chapter 4   Risk & Reward 27

Chapter 5   Buying Mutual Funds 37

Chapter 6   Buying Stocks 49

Chapter 7   Researching on the Internet 63

Chapter 8   Hiring Financial Professionals 73

Chapter 9   Giving Back 83

Workbook 91

Resources, Websites etc 103

Introduction

The Invisible Fence

Have you ever seen a dog try to run through an invisible fence? The pooch usually scrambles to a safe spot under the living room drapes. That's because an electrical cable buried two inches below the ground delivers a shock through a transmitter on the dog's collar. After one zap, even a twitchy tailed squirrel couldn't tempt Fido out of his yard. It isn't meant to be cruel; it protects wandering pets from speeding cars and Cruella de Ville dog nappers.

Life would be easier if we could use invisible fences to rein in our children, except it's generally frowned upon. So, instead of using electrical shocks, we engage another method to keep our offspring in line. It's called social conditioning. If the boundaries are established early on, they can last a lifetime. By the time we're adults, we're so used to the limitations, we often forget that they are there. A few years ago, I stumbled into an invisible fence that I didn't even know existed.

We were standing near the side door at St. Giles on Easter Sunday. The church was packed. The heathens who only surfaced on high holidays had arrived early and staked out entire pews. Ushers squeezed by in red jackets and shrugged apologetically. As more latecomers elbowed in, we shuffled toward the altar. At that moment, the priest waved us forward, motioning for us to step up in order to clear the aisle. Like commuters on a train platform, we herded toward the marble steps. The taste of incense caught in my throat. And then something unexpected happened.

Grade school memories flooded my head. *Girls can't be on the altar. You're in big trouble now.* Like the buried electrical cable, thou-shalt-nots were imprinted just beneath my conscious mind, warning me to retreat to familiar terrain. When I stepped up, I couldn't put my foot down. I could only paw it in the air. Behind me, the wall of bodies pushed forward.

Beads of perspiration trickled down my neck as I finally stood on the altar and tried to sort out my feelings. How could I be carrying around such medieval thinking? Ridiculous. Nowadays there were even altar girls. I closed my eyes and exhaled laboriously, hoping the sound of my breath would chase away the invasive feelings. The world had changed and given me permission to stand on the altar, taking my rightful place in a world once reserved only for men. I couldn't do it and I didn't know why. Obviously I wasn't as liberated as I let on. And then a more disturbing thought pushed its way in. *Were there more invisible fences buried deep inside of me?* I left mass that day with a lot to think about.

We all have invisible fences, different for each of us. Unaware of deep-seated conditioning, especially as it relates to money, many women admit they don't invest and they honestly don't know why.

We're no longer living in the world that once gave us clearly defined roles. Today, women can choose whether or not to marry, have children, pursue a career, or even start up their own businesses. Taking control of their finances can give women meaningful choices in how they want to live their lives and spend their retirement. The would-be investor needs to break through the invisible fence and enjoy her rightful place in the world of money-making. From there, she's free to run as far as she likes.

Chapter 1
Money and Women

Are Women Preconditioned to Avoid Investing?

*I am a marvelous housekeeper.
Every time I leave a man, I keep his house.*
— Zsa Zsa Gabor

"If God had wanted you to wear pants, he would have made you a boy." My mother stood with her hands on her hips by my bedroom closet and frowned as I sat cross-legged on the bed clutching a pair of patched red corduroys to my chest. I was five years old.

Things grew progressively worse. A few years later, my father transformed the attic into a dormer bedroom that my sister and I would share. The bottom half of the wall was painted pink and the top was covered with pink ballerinas that jétéd across the wallpaper. Life-size dancers pirouetted on pink chenille bedspreads draped over twin beds. Out of the closets spilled identical frilly, lacy, and puffed sleeved dresses. Although Angela was two years older, Mom really believed we were twins. My private hell was to inherit Angela's clothes when I outgrew mine.

But having to dress as girls wasn't nearly as unjust, we felt, as being treated like girls. We grumbled as we washed dishes, polished the furniture and vacuumed. Michael and Stephen plugged their thumbs in their ears and waggled their fingers at us as they ran out to play. Mom was raising us to be ladies and housewives. We swore that if we ever had children, the boys would do all the housework. Our two older brothers' chores were manful things like taking out the garbage and cutting the grass. They rarely did either.

So, at a very young age, Angela and I noticed that men were living dramatically different lives than women. My father left in the morning wearing a suit and handed my mother, perpetually stationed at the stove, a paycheck every other Friday. The boys came and went as they pleased. They had big jobs: delivering papers and cutting lawns. They also had dollar bills and coins in their pockets and on their dressers. We noticed that people who earned money didn't clean houses, cook meals, or change stinky diapers. Conversely, those who *didn't* earn money cleaned, cooked and tended to those who did. We deduced that like love, marriage, and baby in a carriage, money, freedom and the male gender went hand-in-hand.

Our upbringing was typical of girls born before the 60's. We were raised deferring to men. Is it any surprise that we would grow up unprepared to voice our opinions, pursue our own dreams, and, most outrageously of all, earn and manage our own money?

However, here we are at the turn of the century and women have more money than ever before. Over half of employed women bring in 50% or more of their household income. One out of three working wives out-earn their husbands. Already, the number of women doctors has doubled, women lawyers have quadrupled, and female officers, from the position of vice president and up in Fortune 500 companies, have almost tripled. Women who were once held back in corporations are now successful entrepreneurs. Soon, over 50 percent of all firms will be female owned. And, according to the media, women are investing in droves. They buy stocks, trade on line, and are financially savvy.

You Don't Have to Be a Bag Lady!
A Humorous Survival Guide for the Reluctant Investor

I have just one question. *Who are these women?*

My friends are professionals with college degrees, but for the most part, they don't invest. Many of them are waking up in midlife, terrified that they have no long-range financial plans. With over 70 million baby boomers hitting their 50's, and half of them women, droves of people will be scrambling to get their financial houses (or cardboard boxes) in order. One friend describes it as spotting a cement truck in her rear view mirror—and it's closing in too fast.

Inflation Eats Savings
Investing Makes Them Grow

It's true that women have always been good in short-range money management. My mother saved for major purchases by hiding a few dollars every payday in one of her secret envelopes. Women are still stashing money away today, but now it's in savings accounts or money markets. These strategies, more or less a variation on the envelope system, barely keep them ahead of inflation.

Since 1926, inflation has averaged 3.1% a year. That doesn't sound like a lot, but, over time, inflation can greatly reduce your purchasing power. What ever happened to penny candy? And how about those dimes we used to tuck into our loafers for a phone call. Chump change. The good news is that if you invest aggressively over time, you will beat inflation and come out way ahead. Look at the return on an investment of $10,000 over 20 years. Cash: $20,900. Bonds: $26,500. Stocks: $72,600.

RULE OF 72

The Rule of 72 will help you determine how many years it will take your money to double at a given interest rate.

Rate of Return	Years to Double
1%	72.0
2%	36.0
3%	24.0
4%	18.0
5%	14.4
6%	12.0
7%	10.3
8%	9.0
9%	8.0
10%	7.2
11%	6.5
12%	6.0
13%	5.5
14%	5.1
15%	4.8
16%	4.5
17%	4.2
18%	4.0
19%	3.8
20%	3.6

Divide 72 by the number of years to estimate the interest rate it will take to double your money. For example, at a rate of 6% your investment will double in 12 years. (72 ÷ 6 = 12) The Rule of 72 can also show how inflation eats away your savings. At a 3% rate of inflation, in 24 years your investment will be worth half of its value. Even 2% inflation will reduce your Savings by 50% in 36 years.

Unfortunately, despite the huge disparity of these numbers, most women continue to go the conservative route with cash or bonds. Investing in stocks over the long term is the better hedge against inflation. Even with their education and ever increasing salaries, women are not protecting themselves financially. Barbara Stanny, author of *Prince Charming isn't Coming*, reports that women are finally in a position to earn money—sometimes a lot of money—but they don't know how to make money work for them, something that will be necessary to see them through their retirement years. They have not learned the power of passive income.

Passive Income

Passive income is really very simple. (Not simple to do, simple to understand) First, you work for your money. You save regularly and sock it away in investments. Your dollars start working slowly, earning interest and appreciating in value. It's difficult in the beginning because watching your money grow is as exciting as waiting for a pot to boil. But over time, your dollars will start percolating. And if you stay on track, someday your dollars will be doing all the work and your only job will be deciding how to spend all of your free time. I have a mental picture of my dollars punching the time clock every day, sweating on the assembly line and cranking out more dollars. Hee. Yah. No vacations. No sick days. Just work, work, work.

But it is only going to happen if you invest consistently and aggressively over many years. Women can be uncompromising and savvy shoppers for groceries, clothes and even a house, but they typically hesitate to purchase intangibles like stocks or mutual funds. Many women confess that when people talk about investments, they feel stupid. They don't understand the language. It's boring and, quite honestly, intimidating. They believe that investing has always been a man's domain, left for their fathers and husbands.

Sheila Peters

Barbara Stanny explains that when women "get stupid" in the midst of financial talk, vocabulary isn't the only barrier. It takes more than mechanics to learn about money. "Factual information does little to change years of conditioning. Women don't think about financial planning because they're waiting for someone to rescue them." Prince Charming can be a man, Social Security benefits, or the winning lottery ticket. It's what my mother called 'your ship coming in'.

But, Angela and I couldn't wait for our ship to come in.

Not only did we want to set sail right then and there, we wanted to be the captains. We decided that the only way to overcome our fate of being girls was to earn our own money. We wanted to jingle the coins in our pockets like the boys.

We followed our older brothers everywhere, hoping to get a glimpse of where they went and what they did in their world. They usually succeeded in ditching us, but oftentimes gave up and just ignored us as we tagged a safe ten feet behind. We'd take any crumbs of enlightenment into the male world.

One of their favorite pastimes was scavenging, or trash-picking as my mother would call it. In those days, all sorts of things that weren't broken or worn out appeared next to garbage cans. Stephen once came home with a perfectly good lawnmower. Sometimes, the item's only offense was that it was no longer useful. More often than not, though, it was just plain ugly.

Angela and I trailed behind them and learned to uncover our own neat things. But at the end of the day, our stash included mostly rejects like cheap flower vases, plastic plants, souvenir ash trays and keychains. Still, every trash day held the promise of being the day we would dig up a treasure.

Mom was less than enthusiastic as we dragged our junk through the kitchen. "Why do you two have to go out there digging around like street urchins? It's so unladylike."

"Michael and Stephen do it," we protested.

"They're boys," she said flatly.

"How come we can't do the stuff they do?" Angela croaked. I stood safely behind her and nodded in support.

Mom turned to poke at something on the stove and said gaily, "Girls do nice things like have tea parties or bake cookies."

"Girls get gypped," Angela yelled over her shoulder. I followed behind as we retreated to the sanctuary of our bedroom. She was still fuming that the Catholic Church wouldn't let girls be altar boys, another male rite of passage. We had transposed her dresser into a church altar using doilies, holy cards and our scavenged vases. As she read passages from her Sunday Missile I would drop to my knees. She flicked homemade holy water on me and placed squashed Wonderbread wafers on my tongue. An old Kleenex box served as the Tabernacle. The dog was our only congregation. All I know is that if he didn't make it to dog heaven, it was his own bloody fault. God only knows how many times he was baptized and blessed, not to mention all the Holy Communions.

Breaking into the Male World

Mom understood that we wanted to make money so we could buy things. But she didn't understand that, for us, making money was a rite of passage into the male world. A world in which girls would not be held back and there would be endless and equal possibilities. She dismissed our money-making schemes, thinking that we would outgrow them. Her job, just like all of our friends' mothers, was to instill in us the qualities that would make us attractive candidates for marriage. Making money was nowhere on that list.

Surprisingly, my father viewed the world very differently from my mother. Quite the idealist, he seemed almost proud of our non-traditional aspirations. Once, Angela asked him what she should be when she grew up. He put down his newspaper, looked thoughtfully at his pipe and said proudly, "I think you could be the first lady president of the United States." She preened like a peacock. "And if you don't want to do that, you could be a lawyer."

Excitedly, I flapped down the basement stairs and peered through the railings where Mom was feeding clothes through the rollers of our ancient washing machine. With each turn of the agitator, the machine danced and jerked around the room on its wheels, slopping water over the rim. She was soaked from the waist down.

"Mom!" I yelled over the churning. "What can I be when I grow up?"

"Well," she said not looking up as a lump of diapers jammed in the rollers and the safety buzzer blared, "You could be a nurse or a teacher. You know, something nice." I crawled back up the stairs. At seven, I was old enough to know I'd been ripped off.

In that same basement, Angela and I piled our scavenged loot. It was a damp, dark, cavernous room that always smelled as if the floodwaters were coming or going, which they usually were. We decided that if we opened a store, people would buy our treasures.

Under a 60-watt light bulb, we set up Mom's square card table and arranged our merchandise. We laboriously snipped a lunchbag into small pieces for price tickets. We strung signs around the trees for two blocks on Mapleton with big arrows — 'TINY'S STORE—OPEN EVERY DAY' — and waited for customers who never came. Except for my father. We'd wait on the front porch until we spotted him walking from the bus stop and lead him down the cracked concrete steps into the dark coolness of Tiny's. He'd slowly scan the table. "Gosh, there's so much to choose from, I don't know what to buy." The jingling of the change in his pocket was like music. He would end up picking some oddball thing and drop a few coins into our Band-Aid can. I would shake it, getting lost in the rattle. We repeated this routine a few more times until we noticed that he would leave his accumulated purchases on his dresser. True scavengers that we were, we began sneaking them back to the basement to replenish our inventory. He never commented when they reappeared on the card table, buying the Blessed Virgin statue again and again, and never tiring of the keychain.

A late summer thunderstorm brought new floodwaters that put Tinys out of business. Mom suggested babysitting. No way. The boys wouldn't be caught dead doing that. We'd think of something else. The bankruptcy of our first venture led us, like any red-blooded entrepreneurs, to our next enterprise.

Sheila Peters

Chapter 2
Money & Love

What's wrong with thinking a man will take care of you?

> *Some people are more turned on by money than they are by love. In one respect they're alike. They're both wonderful as long as they last.*
> — Abigail Van Buren

According to *The Savage Truth on Money*, by Terry Savage, what women fear most is the "bag lady" syndrome. When women look at older women, their role models, they too often see poverty, and for good reason. Today, three-fourths of the elderly poor are women. That could be because half of the women over 65 are divorced or widowed. Eighty percent of women living in poverty were not poor before their husbands died. These women come from a generation that was not encouraged to learn about financial issues, and they had little opportunity to create economic independence. Society taught them a form of learned helplessness. In those days, women depended on men for physical and financial protection, while men depended on women for nesting and emotional nurturing. How could anyone have known that a generation later, everything would change.

Because my mother raised us to believe we would never have to fend for ourselves, she rarely spoke to us about money. However, one night while we were leaning on the kitchen bench watching her make the next day's lunches, she gave us our first financial tidbit. It was a typical weeknight. Five brown bags stood at attention, mouths gaping open, waiting for bologna, egg salad or tuna fish sandwiches. A small bag of Fritos or a Milky Way were thrown in behind to liven things up. Slap. Smear. Wrap. Toss. The job would be ours someday.

She said absently, with a sigh, "When poverty walks in the door, love flies out the window."

Angela and I debated whether the love shouldn't walk and poverty fly. Mom rolled her eyes to the heavens. It wasn't bad enough that she married an engineer. God punished her further with two left-brained daughters who analyzed everything. She was stuck in a house full of realists, a malaise she attributed to Dad's side of the family. Mom's idea of a day well spent was a rainy afternoon nestled on the couch with a cup of hot tea and a lace hankie watching Lawrence Olivier roam the moors in *Wuthering Heights*. A plate of cookies wouldn't be far away. The only romantic advice she bestowed on us was when she chirped, "Remember girls, it's better to be an older man's darling than a young man's slave." We argued that some old coot with one foot in the grave wouldn't do us a lot of good. In the end, we decided that Mom's problem was that she was born too late. Two hundred years too late.

A Bit of History

My mother was raised on a farm in New Zealand and recalls how she fed the newborn lambs with baby bottles. To this day she won't eat mutton; something about sitting at the dinner table and discovering, to her horror, that her lamb, Betty, was that evening's fare. She rode Snowy, an old horse passed from one family to another like a jalopy, to the little convent school nearby. She took piano lessons for seventeen years. After all, isn't that what all young ladies did?

I imagined my mother as a young woman strolling through an English garden wearing a flowing lacy dress with a large sun hat, carefully snipping flowers with her gloved hand and laying them into a basket crooked in her arm. After a modest lunch and a few chapters of Jane Austen, she would settle in with her needlepoint and wait patiently for one of her beaus to ride up in a carriage. Perhaps a note would arrive by dove, secured to its clawed foot by a love interest. Perchance a captain out at sea.

She did meet my father by the sea. The Pacific Ocean to be exact. The year after the bombing of Pearl Harbor, the Americans sent an expeditionary force to New Zealand to invade Guadalcanal which was held by the Japanese. From there the U.S. Forces would work their way toward Japan, invading various Japanese occupied islands. Dad was in the Army Signal Corps. Along with thousands of other New Zealand women, Mom came to the states as a war bride. My father finished his college degree through the GI Bill. They bought a house and settled down to raise a family.

They led a relatively quiet life. After the dinner table was cleared, my father would sit next to my mother and light two cigarettes at one time like Paul Henreid in *Now Voyager*. According to Mom, in her day this was considered quite dashing. On Saturday nights, while Angela and I doled out potato chips and off-brand pop to the crew, my parents watched Lawrence Welk and sipped whiskey sours.

They lived by the rules. Dad brought home the bacon and Mom stretched it to feed ten mouths. He laid down the law and she enforced it. I only remember one time she didn't go along. My friends were going to see the movie *Doctor Zhivago,* but I wasn't allowed to join them because our Catholic newspaper rated it 'for adults only'. After Dad lectured me on the sin of adultery, which sent me rummaging for a dictionary, Mom tiptoed into my bedroom and folded two dollar bills into my hand.

"I want you to see the movie. It's a beautiful love story."

My father died of cancer two years later at the age of forty-nine. My mother was widowed at forty-seven with eight children. She hadn't worked outside the house in over twenty years. Other than a small life insurance policy and the house, there wasn't much else.

Although most women expect to outlive their husbands by a few years, I'm sure Mom assumed she'd be well in her seventies before she'd have to think about that. She was raised to get married and not worry about the possibility that her husband would die or become disabled.

Transition into Independence

When my father was alive, my mother was a wife and a nurturer. When he died she wasn't prepared to become the bread-winner and decision-maker. The relatives thought my mother would go to pieces, but she surprised everyone. Most of all, I think she surprised herself. With quiet determination, she took the $25,000 insurance money and paid off the funeral, mortgage, and bought a reliable car. After a few weeks she took a job as a store clerk. She spent evenings in my brother's room pecking away at his electric typewriter, honing her old secretarial skills. Eventually, she found an office job. It didn't pay much, but it was close to home. She worked there for twenty-six years and never made much more than minimum wage. Because she was grateful to even have a job, she didn't question the low salary. She never saw herself as a "real" wage earner.

Still, after Dad died, Mom emerged as an independent woman. Certainly not overnight, but over the years. She became more assertive and formed her own opinions. She also saw all eight of us through high school and trade schools or college. Some more reluctantly than others, I might add. When Kevin graduated from high school, Mom said they should have given her the diploma for all the times she had to drag him out of bed. It would have been easier to have just taken the classes herself.

Had Mom been born at a different time, she might have thought about getting a college education to increase her own possibilities and income. But she was just like most women of her generation. She was raised to depend on someone else. Barbara Stanny, author of *Prince Charming Isn't Coming*, explains that if a woman becomes financially independent, she no longer needs a man in the traditional sense. This could be perceived as threatening to men. "If they remain ladylike and needy, someone will take care of them. Women associate financial rescue or living happily ever after with satisfaction of other emotional needs. They are afraid that abandoning the rescue fantasy also means abandoning the possibility of love." A gentleman caller who was financially solid would be welcome in any family's parlor to court one of their daughters. But woe be the woman who earned too much of her own money—a most unfeminine malady.

Fear of the Future

Our family's experience wasn't all that unique. Many women have watched their fathers die and their mothers struggle just to get by. (Women outlive their mates by seven years on average.) They or their parents got divorced or they watched a friend go through it. And the statistics are as encouraging as a red flag on a slick mountain road. People are staying single longer, half of all marriages are ending in divorce, and more people are living together unmarried. At some point in their lives, ninety percent of women will be solely responsible for their finances.

Furthermore, the average woman's standard of living drops 45% in the first year after a divorce, while a man's actually rises 15%. Women no longer benefit as much in property settlements and there is a growing tendency to cap or end alimony payments. Baby Boomers can't get too comfortable with the safety net of Social Security. There may not be enough generation X'ers to fund it. Increasingly, the responsibility for retirement income is moving from the government and employer to the individual.

Sheila Peters

When I hear these statistics, my legs turn to rubber. I look in the hall mirror and ask, *What will become of me?* I have no kids, although that's no guarantee. Who's to say they wouldn't throw me in a nursing home and declare me incompetent. I reassure myself that one of my siblings will take me in. If they turn me away, they'll roast in hell (or at least have to deal with my mother in the afterlife). A picture looms in my mind. I'm living in one of their basements stooped over a 2-burner stove stirring my gruel. I scrub floors and wash and iron their clothes. A bandana scrapes back my hair as beads of sweat roll down my face. The cat skulks down the stairs and glares at me territorially as he crouches in front of his bowl. *Poof.* The nightmare disappears. I shake my head wondering why I have these thoughts. After all, I am financially secure.

Gail Sheehy, author of *New Passages,* reports that, "The prevalence of bag-lady fears, particularly among professional women who are beyond economic dependence on a man, is really quite astonishing." Financial planning is new to our generation of women. However, despite the progress we have made, we are still struggling with the fear that we are not capable of controlling our financial destinies. Why do we feel that way?

Gender Attitudes Toward Money

Money Magazine reports that men see money as a flow that just keeps on coming while women see it as a pool that can be drained empty. In part, this is because men typically have greater earning power than women. Many women will be in and out of the workforce due to raising children or taking care of aging parents. Women not only work in lower paying jobs, they still tend to be paid 60% to 80% of what men earn for doing the same job. The fact that women are much less confident than men about their earning power affects many of their financial decisions. Because men are confident about their earning power, they find it easier to make large purchases. They are much more willing to take risks with money than are women. But, now that so many women are earning good salaries, it's time that they close the investment gap and start taking some investing risks.

Some married women feel they don't need to worry about earning power and investment risks. Their husbands have taken care of all of that. But, they still need to get involved in their marital finances. Terry Savage says that women need to understand their rights to Social Security benefits and pension plans under their husband's accounts. She suggests these steps for all women, whether married, divorced or single.

1. Start and contribute to your own retirement plan. Even non-working spouses can put up to $2,000 in an IRA every year.
2. Set aside and manage your own money even if most of your assets are contributed to a joint checking account.
3. Women in the midst of divorce should always get their own financial adviser so they are left with the right assets.
4. Women whose spouses are retiring should never sign off to reject widow's benefits in favor of a larger current check while the husband is still alive.

Years later when we could talk openly about my father's death, I asked Mom, "If you could have said one last thing to Dad, what would it have been?" With no hesitation she replied, "I'd say, 'Lee, how could you have left me in such financial straits? Raising all those children with no money.'"

Sheila Peters

Chapter 3
Money & Power

Don't women realize that money gives them choices?

> *Money can't buy happiness, but it sure can buy the kind of misery you prefer.*
> —Unknown

My mother taught us about budgeting with four words, "We can't afford that." And if she was especially trying to make her point she would add, "What do you think this is? Guy Fawkes Day?" Supposedly, Guy Fawkes was a bloke who tried to burn down Parliament in the 1600's and was subsequently sent to the gallows. Because New Zealand was a commonwealth of England, they celebrate the foiled attempt each year with celebrations and fireworks.

On the subject of money itself, we learned from the boys. My brothers and their buddies always had paper routes. Many mornings I awoke to the familiar cursing of eighth grade boys, followed by the kitchen window shooting up, my mother's proper voice piercing through the dark, "Tut, tut. We'll have none of that vulgarity in this house."

I would look longingly down from my bedroom window, beyond the white fenced yard, past the sandbox and swing set, where they were rolling that morning's edition of the *Chicago Tribune*. Michael snatched a paper from a waist-high pile, folded it in half twice, banded it, and tossed it over his head. A growing pyramid was taking shape in the battered cart. The sun was just inching over the garage, but the agency had dropped off the papers hours before.

Sheila Peters

They were paid $20 a month for 200 papers delivered daily. I gazed wishfully at the list of chores taped to the refrigerator. The fourth line read: dishes, sweep kitchen floor-25¢. I calculated it would take roughly the same time to save $20 as the time needed for a rocket ship to reach Pluto. During one of our brainstorming sessions, Angela and I decided we would split a route. Dad wouldn't even hear of it.

"Now what makes you think we'd let you roam the streets in the dark? Certainly not."

Mom wasn't any better. "Why the neighbors would think we'd lost our minds."

"But you let Michael and Stephen do it," we cried.

"That's different. They're boys." Dad sucked on his pipe and disappeared behind his paper.

Angela muttered her usual refrain, "Girls get gypped," as we withdrew to our bedroom. I flopped on my bed, but not before reclaiming yesterday's gum from the headboard. She dug out a Folger's Coffee can buried deep in her dresser drawer. Three quarters, a dime, and two nickels bounced on the bed. A worn dollar bill floated out. It was our first taste of adolescent injustices that we would not understand for many years.

That winter dumped Chicago with record snow and with it our next enterprise. Dad agreed that most people would pay a dollar to have their walks shoveled, but the boys couldn't be bothered. Peering out our window before bed, we prayed for snow. I kept my rosary nestled under my pillow. Surely the Blessed Virgin knew how we felt. Without snow, we were doomed to pennies and nickels.

Money Conditioning

People are finally realizing that in our society men and women are conditioned almost from birth to view money in different ways. A recent survey conducted for Girls Incorporated, a 52-year-old nonprofit organization dedicated to girls' personal growth, revealed that girls lag behind boys in confidence and knowledge in money matters. Girls were more hesitant than boys to learn how to make money in the stock market. The girls also said they would be less likely to invest their money and would invest smaller sums of it than boys.

The study also revealed that 50% of girls learn about financial issues from their mothers compared to 27% who look to their fathers for financial guidance. They found that many mothers don't feel prepared for this responsibility. Three-quarters of the women said they wished they had learned more about money when they were growing up.

In our society, men often see money as representing status or power. Conversely, women tend to see money as providing security. Phyllis Chesler, author of *Women, Money & Power*, says that "Even if we perceive it metaphorically as freedom, security, love, or happiness, the profound truth that women, in particular, need to understand is: Money means power. Money, in and of itself, does not give us power. Money bestows power by giving us choices."

Delivering the News

Itching for that power, without yet knowing it was the path to choice, my sister and I discovered there were afternoon routes for the *Chicago Daily News*. These routes were much smaller and required no collecting of money from subscribers. Whols' Newspaper Agency was a short walk from home.

"Go on in. It was your idea."

"Don't push me." Angela gnawed on what was left of her iodine stained nails. Mom was determined to rid her of the unladylike habit.

I sat on a concrete stoop, three doors away, while Angela paced back and forth. We were wearing one of our twin outfits- red peddle pushers with sleeveless shirts dotted with multicolored popsicles. The office was a flurry of activity as delivery trucks screeched to a stop, dropped bundles of papers at the curb, and drove away. Newspaper boys ran in and out. We lost our nerve but returned early the next morning to find the office quiet. Only Whols was in the room, sitting at his desk. Gray paint peeled from the wall in what was once a green room. I could do no more than peer through the dusty glass and chew on one of my braids. Angela opened the door and walked up to him. When he removed his cigar and shook his head, my heart fell. But Angela ran out excited, slapping the screen door against the building.

"He said to come back later in the week. Some guy is quitting!" We wiggled into a hula dance, oblivious to the glances of early morning commuters.

When we left Whols' office the next time, Angela was carrying a deck of 30 address cards bound with a large silver ring while I held a box of rubberbands close to my chest. It smelled like a new bicycle tire. The afternoon route had thirty papers. Three o'clock each day found us bounding home from school to smartly snap rubber bands on that day's edition, our hands blackened like seasoned veterans. We split the route in half and took off in different directions. At least once a week we tortured Dad with, "What's black and white and red all over?"

"Gosh, I don't know," he feigned every time.

"Dad, a *newspaper*, get it?"

He fastened front baskets on our bikes and we learned to ride and throw. Normally the agency gave you one extra paper which was a relief because the ones on the roof looked like they'd be up there for a while.

On the last day of the month, we galloped all the way to the agency. This time I pushed my way in with Angela. Whols handed us a small yellow envelope and smiled. "Nice job, girls. Wish I had more like you." He was no dummy. He knew girls were more reliable than boys. He didn't care if Dumbo the Elephant flew in to deliver the papers, as long as they got there on time. To the casual observer, we looked like blossoming feminists. But we weren't interested in women's rights—only our rights or at least our share of the action.

We agreed to wait until we got home to look at the money. As we sat cross-legged on Angela's bed, she opened the packet slowly. We took turns looking in. A five-dollar bill and two quarters rested at the bottom. We could taste the power. I spent my share as fast as I could race the three blocks to Jim's Dairy Store and slap my coins on the counter in exchange for candy. Angela sealed every dime into her coffee can. We would retain these polar money attitudes for many years. In my mind, money management meant spending it faster than my brothers could manage to lift it off my dresser while I was sleeping. Hiding anything in our house was futile.

Girls and Money

Terry Savage explains in *The Savage Truth on Money* that women develop their money personalities as young girls. These are a reflection of the cultural beliefs that were in vogue when they were young. Angela and I were caught between two worlds. In Mom's world, money issues were willingly yielded over to men. In our brothers' world, money bought freedom. My sister and I couldn't understand why women would settle for such a crummy deal.

But our paper route was a good deal and helped level a few bumps in the playing field. Although the pay was meager, Christmas tips were a bonanza. The Christmas Eve edition appeared on our curb along with 30 calendars that read, *Merry Christmas from your paperboy*. We lined out *boy* with a red pen and printed *girl* above it.

"OK," Angela explained, "we ring the doorbells, hand them the paper and calendar and say 'Merry Christmas'".

"Then what?" I asked, confused.

"They give us a tip," she beamed.

"I'm not doing that. We'll look stupid just standing there."

Sheila Peters

"OK, chicken. You hand them the paper and I'll do the talking."

And sure enough, by that evening, she lay 27 rumpled one-dollar-bills on her dresser. Three people were not home; she was holding their papers hostage until Christmas morning when we would go back.

When I was ten, I found a route of my own, leaving Angela the original route until a few years later, fearing that tossing papers wouldn't look cool for an incoming freshman, she willed it back to me. But always the wheeler dealer, she argued that she should get 75% of the Christmas tips since she had worked three quarters of the year. She nearly strangled me when she discovered that I had rolled the calendars inside the papers and simply dropped them at people's front doors. A few kind souls left me envelopes. She insisted on default money, but I refused.

"Go ring the bloody doorbells yourself. I'm not doing it!"

When I reached high school, I bequeathed the route to my brother Mark. Out of eight kids, six of us had it spanning at least fifteen years. Some more than once. It was passed around like the butter dish. But so many complaints and cancellations came in when Kevin, the youngest boy took over, that within a year the entire route liquidated. But this wasn't before my mother ended up delivering the papers herself to fend off annoyed neighbors.

My sister and I never had a single complaint or missed a day of delivery. So we couldn't understand why Mom nagged the boys out of bed in the morning to wrap the papers for their morning route, waking the rest of us in the process. Some mornings when I heard the rubber bands snap and pop in the back porch, I knew it was Mom in her bathrobe wrapping the papers. You could always tell the ones she had banded, all lopsided and fat.

"A man on a galloping horse wouldn't know the difference," she'd always retort. Mom never commented on our route, but I think deep down she was afraid we would show up the boys.

You Don't Have to Be a Bag Lady!
A Humorous Survival Guide for the Reluctant Investor

Many years later she confessed, "I never worried about you two. You girls were always go-getters. It's the boys who needed that extra push."

I wasn't alone in my ignorance. Most parents don't expose their daughters to money management. However, there are ways to shape their money IQ. Girls Inc. has these tips for raising financially savvy girls:

1. Decide together how much of chores-allowance should be spent or saved for later.
2. Openly discuss family finances. Financial planning is a part of everyday life.
3. Debunk the myth of Prince Charming.
4. Encourage interests that lead to careers.
5. Use the Sunday classified ads to talk about salaries, the cost of renting an apartment and buying a car.
6. Watch TV together and discuss images of wealth and gender. Are rich and successful female characters portrayed as friendly and productive, or are they greedy and self-centered?
7. Discuss how advertisements try to convince you to buy products.
8. Encourage girls in math.
9. Play an investment game together. Pretend to buy shares of a stock in a store or restaurant she likes. Watch it grow and/or decline and graph it over time.

Sheila Peters

Chapter 4
Risk & Reward

Can you learn without making mistakes?

> *Ginger Rogers did everything Fred Astaire did,*
> *but she did it backwards and in high heels.*
> — Faith Whittlesey

According to Esther Berger, author of *Money Smart*, chronic financial paralysis among women "has been created and perpetuated, generation after generation, by the belief that financial know-how involves secret, mysterious knowledge intrinsic to men. That there are, in fact, money secrets men never tell women."

The only real money secret that men don't share with women is that many of them are just as confused. We assume that men know about finance because they've been told from day one that they will have to handle the money. Until recently, both genders have accepted that. But times have changed and circumstances are forcing women to take the reins. Many women are now the sole breadwinners in their families. In their defense, many men are no more capable or interested in money management and investing than are some women. They too wish, secretly, that someone else would do the dirty deed.

Women need to realize that money knows no gender. Money doesn't care whose pocket it's in, a man's or a woman's. Knowledge is what determines how full that pocket gets. Even though women collectively earn less than men, when it comes to investing, a woman's investing power is equal to a man's and can even overcome the smaller income barrier. It's the lack of knowledge that holds women back; they can smell the possibility of failure. Stepping into the male financial arena takes guts, or at least the ability to hide your fear. But, once you have the knowledge, you realize that it levels that old playing field. My sister and I learned that when we had a Good Humor route.

Finding the Humor

During high school, we spent our summers at office jobs. Thanks to the thousands of newspapers we banded, we had agile fingers and quickly became fast typists. But one particular summer, Angela decided to forgo the confinement of an office job. Instead, she got a Good Humor route selling ice cream.

Anticipating that working the route every day would be exhausting, she asked me to drive on Sundays. I thought it would be a nice break from my office job, so I agreed to ride with her on Saturday to learn the ropes. How hard could it be? Selling ice cream bars to little kids.

As I sat in the truck in the Good Humor yard, wearing bellbottom jeans, a white shirt and matching brimmed hat, the promise of excitement tingled up my spine. Through the rear view mirror, I spotted Angela walking from the office. I smoothed sun tan lotion on my arms as I waited. The other drivers were already lined up to fill their trucks with ice cream.

Fifty feet ahead, a deep freezer billowed out steam as three figures in silver quilted suits trudged forward pushing carts heavy with popsicles and ice cream cones. The temperature was already eighty. As they wheeled toward the crowd of Good Humor drivers, ready to trade product for money, the lead spaceman removed his mittens and head cover. Drivers of every imaginable nationality swarmed around him. It sounded like the Tower of Babel.

"Hey guys, one at a time!" he screamed, backing away. The drivers barked and shoved to hold their places. A slightly built driver with a straggly pony tail trailing down his back was squeezed out of the circle.

You Don't Have to Be a Bag Lady!
A Humorous Survival Guide for the Reluctant Investor

I turned to Angela. "Is this safe?"

"Sure," she waved her hand in the air a bit too confidently. "We've got as much right to be here as they do." We watched as the first drivers filled their freezers and filed out in a procession of shiny white vehicles. Our truck was a rusted '58 Ford with a manual transmission. Through the layers of grime, someone had fingered 'wash me' on its side. Newer trucks were awarded to drivers with the highest sales. Out of thirty drivers, my sister and another girl were the only females. Her truck had a big dent in the front. Since there was only one seat in our truck, I agreed to sit on the floor if I could wear the metal coin changer. A worn steering wheel was all that separated Angela from the pitted windshield.

When all the other trucks had left and a quiet settled over the yard, Angela crunched into first gear and inched toward the spacemen. She stopped the truck a few feet from them and got out.

"Excuse me," she said politely. "We'd like to buy some ice cream." One of the spacemen leered at us through mirrored sunglasses with a smile that disclosed perfectly shaped teeth, whiter yet for his jet black moustache. All we were missing was 'suburbs' stamped on our foreheads.

"Only rocket bars left. Want 'em?"

"Yeah, we'll take them all." She fingered through her money pouch and held out five ten-dollar-bills while I shrank back. Her hand was shaking. He eased two singles from the inside of a banded wad of one-hundred dollar bills. We hurried to fill the truck with the left over inventory, most of it crushed and dented. I could feel his eyes scanning us as he leaned on the freezer door, rolling a cigarette between his fingers. Our freezer stocked, we set off to make our fortune in rocket bars.

Angela didn't realize until summer's end that drivers negotiated price on damaged goods. Not even out of the yard and we had already lost money.

Sheila Peters

Mistake #1: *With any investment, it's important to know what you're buying.*

Each time we hit a pothole, the truck lifted in the air. It was like driving through a mine field. The pavement rolled past our doorless chariot as I hung onto a metal bar. As Angela scraped through the gears, I wondered if our truck would make it through the day.

"Are we taking the expressway?" I asked.

"Well, here's the deal," she said. "We take it and chance overheating, or we get on Roosevelt Road."

"And be lucky if we're only robbed? I vote for the expressway. At least there's cops out there."

We drove 40 miles-an-hour down the expressway hovering in the right lane. Angela sat high on the seat with her hair tucked under her hat. Her long legs barely skimmed the pedals. She looked as if she was steering a hubcap.

"You can drive when we get there," she said staring ahead.

A panic swept over me. "I can't drive stick. I don't know how!"

"So tomorrow you're going to park the truck outside of the Good Humor yard and wait for people to come to you?"

I sheepishly fiddled with the coin changer, clicking out dimes and slipping them back into the slots.

In spite of her white knuckles, she said, "Don't worry. It's easy, I taught myself." I squeezed my eyes shut as an oil truck glided into our lane, just feet in front of us. We misread the map and overshot our exit, all the while squabbling over who was the navigator. A ride that should have taken thirty minutes took us almost two hours.

Mistake #2: *In any venture, you need a step-by-step plan to reach your goals.*

You Don't Have to Be a Bag Lady!
A Humorous Survival Guide for the Reluctant Investor

When we finally arrived in our territory, the streets were deserted. "Ring the bell," Angela said. "Maybe they're all inside." I could just reach the cord from where I sat on the floor with my feet dangling inches above the street *jingle, jingle.* As it rang, my mind tumbled back to hot summer nights of empty mayonnaise jars filled with grass reeds and lightning bugs. Our ears would strain for the Good Humor bell, dimes creased in our hands. "I hear him. He's coming." Kids, dogs and bicycles would pound down the street. We all wanted the blue popsicles, the ones that tasted like toothpaste. By the time Art the Good Humor man reached our block, there were usually none left.

Art was the neighborhood hero. He looked like Zorro with his pencil thin moustache. From my seven-year-old height, his white uniform and glistening metal changer filled me with awe and respect. Coins slid through his fingers like magic. Some nights he didn't come, but worse yet were the nights when there was another driver. "Art's coming back, isn't he?" we'd all plead. Sometimes we'd sit on the porch until late at night, never giving up. Was he nearby or were those far off jingles just imagined?

I jolted back to reality when the truck leaned hard to the left and Angela tried to downshift. In the side mirror I caught a glimpse of little arms and legs. As the truck came to a halt, two boys ran laughing, their arms filled with ice cream bars. Vapor poured from the freezer door and rocket bars lay strewn on the street, a trail to the villains. Angela chased them as I crawled around, salvaging what I could. In the darkness of the freezer, our two Coke cans had exploded. The inside was caked in blobs of frozen carbonation.

"You rotten kids, get outa here! Next time, we'll run ya over!" She threw a broken popsicle in their general direction. We didn't know that the experienced drivers put locks on their freezer doors. I tied my bandanna through the door handle to protect our remaining inventory.

Sheila Peters

Mistake #3: *Always evaluate your risk of loss so you can minimize it.*

One thing many investors are discouraged to learn is that even if you do your homework, there are risks involved in investing. You can't make money without the element of risk. In the investment world, risk can determine return. The potential profits are directly related to the amount of risk you are willing to take. Despite all your hard work, there are four potential outcomes when you buy investments.

1. You *do* your homework and your investment goes *up*.
2. You *do* your homework and your investment goes *down*.
3. You *don't* do your homework and your investment goes *up*.
4. You *don't* do your homework and your investment goes *down*.

Numbers three and four are no different than gambling. Of course, you can get a wild stock tip and make money, but your stocks can just as easily plunge. Doing your homework is the only way to build your investments over the long run so that the ups and downs are smoothed out.

You have to be willing to feel uncomfortable and make mistakes while you are learning. There's no way around it. Peter Lynch, author of *Beating the Street*, understands how amateur investors can feel intimidated. "Stock stars are treated like rock stars." Many new investors fear that they can't possibly hope to successfully invest without an MBA degree. But, doesn't it seem funny how Wall Street analysts have all the answers the day after stock prices go up or down? Why didn't anyone see the market correction of October 1987. How about the tech wreck in 2000? The truth is that no one really knows what's going to happen in the market. Not only are the experts often off target, but they charge tremendous fees and give no refunds.

Learning about investing money is a skill that you develop. You don't need to be a genius or have a special talent. You just need to get started. The more knowledge women gain about investing, the more they realize that there is no mystique. Terry Savage compares learning about money to how we learn to raise children—by reading books, talking to friends in a similar situation, and improving our success rate based on our instincts and experience. Doing your homework and learning about money, one step at a time, is the way to build confidence and security for the future.

Getting Educated

There are many ways to get started in your financial education. Sign up for financial planning seminars, workshops and lectures. Join an investment club. Watch the business news. Surround yourself with women who are interested in learning about investing. Ask lots and lots of questions. Learning occurs in small increments, day by day. Only later, when you look over your shoulder, will you realize how much more you know.

Angela and I thought we had done our Good Humor homework by memorizing the prices and flavors, but it wasn't enough. We were sorely lacking in street smarts.

Mistake #4: *Investment smarts only come over time through experiencing risk and reward.*

If you're committed to investing over the long haul, you can endure the inevitable lean years. Realize that over time, stocks have averaged a 11% increase per year. According to *A Woman's Guide to Investing*, by Virginia Morris and Kenneth Morris, investors face a 28% chance of losing money in any given year. However, over 10 years, the risk dropped to 2%.

Sheila Peters

Although Angela and I were taking risks, we seemed to be experiencing only the downside. While driving around we spotted a softball game at a park. But there was already a Good Humor truck at the curb with a group of boys buzzing around it.

"He's pirating our area. He can't do that!" I protested .

We slowly pulled up behind him and spied from our truck. When he looked up and bared his teeth at us, we zoomed away, consoling ourselves with the most mangled rocket bars. We could have confronted him, but leaving was probably the smartest move we made all day. We discarded the territory map and drove aimlessly. By three o'clock, the temperature on the bank's sign read 102 degrees. Our shirts were now a palette of soda, rocketbar, and dirt stains.

I looked at my sister. "You look terrible."

"You think you look any better? At least I still have a hat." Mine had been sucked out hours ago on the expressway. We pulled into a gas station and felt new life as we bird-bathed in the ladies room. I made a mental note to bring a towel the next day as I peeled the wet tissue paper off my face.

When it was my turn to drive, I nervously perched myself on the driver's seat. To get a feel for the manual transmission, I held down the clutch and shifted through the gears. It was like grinding rocks together. When I gave it gas, the truck lurched forward and died, pitching us both into the windshield.

"Not so fast! You're going to kill us."

On my third try, the truck inched forward, shaking and sputtering. Taking a leap of faith, I floored the accelerator and popped up the clutch. We were off.

By evening, it was apparent that we had too many rocketbars and popsicles, but not enough of the new fangled Good Humor bars shown on the glossy pictures outside of the truck. By the time we had filled our truck that morning, the more aggressive drivers had already cleaned out the novelty ice cream bars.

You Don't Have to Be a Bag Lady!
A Humorous Survival Guide for the Reluctant Investor

Mistake #5: *With any investment, you need to diversify, not putting all your eggs in one basket.*

By the end of the day, I felt like a veteran and showed off by making change without even looking. It seemed funny, how afraid I had been that morning in the Good Humor yard. The difference was that now I had more than intellectual knowledge. I had a working knowledge of the truck and the job. I even had some ideas on improvements. If we could call the township and find out when and where there were festivals or events, we could increase sales. Filling the freezer the night before would increase our chances of a broader product selection and get us out of the yard earlier. After learning the basics, we could now move on to the next level.

It is the same with investing. Reading books and talking with people are a good start, but eventually, you have to put your own oar in the water. Buying only one stock or mutual fund will open the door to understanding. As you track your investment, you'll start noticing newspaper and magazine articles about the company. You'll click your heels when the stock price zigs up and learn to stay calm when it zags down. Remember, you're in it for the long haul. Barbara Stanny, author of *Prince Charming Isn't Coming*, points out that there are 7 things to keep in mind when investing.

1. Trust your intuition
2. Learn from your mistakes
3. Go slow
4. Start small
5. Invest regularly
6. Diversify broadly
7. Know what you're buying

Do your homework and build a portfolio with stocks of companies you have researched. Look at their performance over the past ten years. Buy and hold—even the pros can't time the market. If, after doing your homework, the thought of risk turns your legs to Jello, the stock market isn't the place for you. Put your dough in a money market. But, remember, *the biggest risk you can take is taking no risk at all.*

There was another area in which Angela and I failed to do our homework. Because we assumed that we would be reimbursed for the broken popsicles, we ate them all. Sometimes taking just one bite and tossing them out the window. We found out later that they had to be returned for a refund. No write-off for depreciation of popsicles.

Mistake #6: *Don't make assumptions. Ask.*

At ten o'clock, with an empty freezer, we headed home. The cool expressway breeze gently massaged us. An hour later, the truck wheezed out a final cough as we chugged into the Good Humor lot. The hard-core drivers had not only beaten us back, but had left again with full freezers. Too exhausted to drive, I handed her the keys to Mom's car. We'd been out for twelve hours and made a profit of $30.

"Angela, I don't think I'm cut out for this."

I kept my promise and drove the next day, but discovered that I didn't enjoy driving alone. I preferred the camaraderie of working with others. I also wasn't comfortable getting paid on commission. Too risky for my blood. By late afternoon, like an old horse heading back to the barn, the truck seemed to turn itself around and point in the direction of the Good Humor yard. I didn't fight it. I'd had enough of the Good Humor experience to know that it wasn't for me. The same goes for investing styles. Some people like to go it alone while others prefer investment clubs. Some investors are energized by risk; others shrink from it. You won't know your limitations and preferences until you take the first step. And the next. And the next.

Chapter 5
Buying Mutual Funds

Why are stock funds a good way to begin investing?

> *Money doesn't grow on trees; you've got to beat the bushes for it.*
> —Anonymous

Women still invest too little and too late, according to a recent *Money Magazine* article. One reason is that they generally have less money to put away. Despite women's 52% majority in the workplace, they earn 71¢ for every $1 earned by their male counterparts. Worse, 6 out of 10 women working today do not have pension plans (vs. 5 out of 10 men). This is more reason, yet, for women to learn about investing. Mutual funds are a great place to begin if you don't have a lot of money or time to invest. When you buy a mutual fund you are contributing to a large pool of money that a fund manager uses to buy investments such as stocks and bonds.

Mutual funds have been around for decades, but became quite popular in the early 90's. In 2000, there were more than 10,000 mutual funds containing $3.7 trillion in assets, excluding money market funds. Some people say that mutual funds are for chickens. But, if that's true, a lot of people are clucking all the way to the bank. Sure, it sounds cool to say you own stocks, but the plain truth is that most of us just aren't willing to do the work involved in buying individual stocks. It takes a lot of time to research them. Besides, buying individual stocks doesn't necessarily mean you'll make more money.

Sheila Peters

I buy mutual funds because portfolio managers and researchers look at the market every day. I'm not willing to do that. Also, funds offer instant diversification that I could only get if I owned a lot of different stocks. I can't afford to do that. Finally, my mutual fund company deducts the same amount each month from my checking account to buy more shares of my existing funds. I'm not disciplined enough to do that. Investing $50 a month ($600/year), at 8%, over 25 years will yield $47,551.

Mutual funds allow unsavvy investors like me to get in on the action and still have a life.

Shopping for Funds

When I first started looking at mutual funds years ago, I spotted an article in *USA Today* touting the success of Fidelity Investments. It listed all their stock mutual funds. I went to the local Fidelity office with my dog-eared article and sat down with a representative. Back then, they were not permitted to recommend specific funds, but the man did help me rank them from conservative to aggressive. I nodded as he pointed out that some were growth funds and others were value funds. It was all Greek to me. In the end, I selected six funds and scribbled out a check. It was strangely like peering over a deli counter and pointing, *I'll take one of those, and, oh yes, two of those over there*.

After four years, my funds had grown considerably. Had I simply picked the right stocks? Or was I like the proverbial monkey flinging darts at a target of fund names which in the end, fared as well or better than those picked by Wall Street gurus? Considering how well the stock market had performed and how little I knew, the monkey, had he accompanied me to Fidelity, would today, probably be living in a penthouse in New York City. (Provided, of course, that he had the foresight to cash in on his Internet stocks before they bombed) But, had I waited to get educated, I would have missed five terrific years in the stock market. Nevertheless, I was tormented with the thought that, had I known what I was doing, I might have done even better. I set off on a mission to get educated.

I began by reading *A Common Sense Guide to Mutual Funds* by Mary Rowland. She points out that there are actually three types of mutual funds: stock, bond, and money market.

Stock Funds

When people speak about mutual funds, they are usually talking about stock mutual funds. A share of stock represents a share of ownership in a company and its profits. A stock fund is typically a collection of stock shares of many companies. Stock funds may be risky, but because they invest in the stock of 50 to 200 companies, they are not as risky as investing in individual stocks. Over time, these funds often provide the greatest earnings potential. These are for people who like to run with the bulls, whether on Wall Street or the streets of Pamplona, Spain. Sometimes both. Stock funds make money for you by paying dividends from their profits, capital gains distributions, and appreciation in price.

Bond Funds

Bonds are loans issued by corporations or government agencies. Bonds pay out interest at a stated rate for a set period of time (years). The principle is usually paid back at the end of the term. Income from bond funds can be reinvested in the fund or paid to you in regular checks. They are different than money markets in that bond funds invest in longer-term securities and are subject to both interest rate risk and credit risk. They typically have a lower yield than stock funds, but higher than money market funds. As interest rates fall, bond values often increase. Conversely, as interest rates increase, bonds can decrease in value. Bonds tend to appeal to the more conservative investors. These funds are for people who would rather cross country ski than downhill. Why risk the fall? What's the hurry?

Money Market Funds

These are also in the mutual fund family. These funds operate like a bank savings account except they have a higher yield. This is the only type of mutual fund whose share price does not fluctuate in value. Costs are locked in at $1 per share. The money is invested conservatively and pays dividends. Your investment is liquid and withdrawals can be made from a personal checking account. Money markets are for investment couch potatoes. After all, if they don't leave the couch, they can't get hurt. But the world (and the lost interest) passes them right by.

Some investors fast forward to the couch potato category when they learn that mutual funds are not backed by federal or state agencies in the way that the Federal Deposit Insurance Corp. guarantees bank deposits. However, the mutual fund industry is regulated by the U.S. Securities and Exchange Commission which requires mutual funds to disclose information about their fees, past performance, and portfolio investments.

As I invested over time, I became more comfortable taking some risks. Generally, the greater an investment's potential return, the greater its risk. I began to diversify so that when some of my investments were down in value, chances are good that the others were up. I also had to evaluate my time horizon, which is the length of time I expected to keep my money in a fund to enjoy a good return. Aggressive funds require a longer holding time because of greater volatility which increases the risk of losing money over the short term .

Even if you know what you're doing, which excluded me, investing can play tricks on your mind. When the stock market was doing well, I kicked myself for not having dumped more money into stock funds. However, when there was a significant market correction, I couldn't remember why investing had ever seemed like a sane idea. Why hadn't I just stuffed it all in a shoebox under my bed?

I discovered that many mutual funds come in families, which is a group of funds with different objectives that are distributed by one management company. Just like any family, there are all sorts of characters. In addition to the stars, you've got loafers, braggers, and underperformers. Then, of course, you always have those middle-of-the-road dependables. Your biggest job will be to decide just which one you're dealing with. The largest fund companies are Fidelity and Vanguard. You can usually switch funds within the particular management company at no charge. Too bad it's not as easy to switch relatives.

Index Funds

Having read several articles about the success and low expense fees of index funds, I was getting the itch to buy one. The goal of an index fund is to produce the same results as the index it tracks. For instance, buying a fund that tracks the Standard & Poor's 500 Index means that you will own all 500 large company stocks traded in that index. The Wilshire 5000 is an index of all stocks on all exchanges in the U.S.(over 6,000 stocks) The Russell 2000 tracks 2000 small company U.S.stocks. Index funds have some of the lowest expenses because they do not require ongoing research like other funds. An index fund manager passively invests to match the performance of an index and the computer pretty much runs the show. And, less buying and selling in the fund mean lower taxes for you.

I called Fidelity to compare their Spartan Market Index Fund with the popular Vanguard Index 500. The customer service person clearly explained the different management expenses and minimum deposits. Once it became evident that the representative was knowledgeable, I asked her if my portfolio of funds was diversified enough.

She said, "Well, first tell me how experienced you are in investing?" I froze, fearing she would see that I knew less than the dart-flinging monkey. How truthful did I have the courage to be?

When in Mexico - Lesson #1

I flashed back to a vacation in Mexico that I had taken with a girlfriend. Our first hour in Mexico City, we wandered into a restaurant. When the waiter approached our table, I said confidently with a wave of my hand, '*Uno frio cervasa, pour favor*', the extent of my Spanish. We said this back home at the local watering hole after our softball games. I just *had* to say it to someone in Mexico. However, noting the mastery of my one sentence, the waiter took off in a streak of Spanish. Despite my protests of *'No Englais'*, he kept jabbering, pausing periodically for my response, which amounted to nothing more than a blank stare. I discovered that pretending I knew more than I did was not a great idea. I quickly drew a hamburger on my napkin that looked more like a flying saucer.

With a picture of that waiter in my mind, I responded hesitantly to the lady at Fidelity, "Am I an experienced investor? Well, kinda, sorta...not really." My face felt very hot.

She went on to say that my portfolio was well balanced and an index fund would be duplicating many of the stocks that I already owned. She answered my tax questions and was patient when I stumbled, "Gosh, it's hard hearing over these cheap portable phones. Could you repeat that a third time?" I could barely read my own chicken scratch.

I was also hot on the trail to find out about a fund of funds, which is just as its name says—a combination of mutual funds within a fund. I was surprised to learn that one of my funds already had other funds in it. I was even more surprised that the customer service person didn't try to sell me anything. After that, I began using their toll-free customer service to help me make decisions.

Mutual Funds Aren't all the Same

All mutual funds have different objectives and different risks. You will need to determine which ones are right for you.

Growth funds invest in stocks in public companies that are growing and are expected to increase in value. Growth funds are usually for long-term investors who can handle the ups and downs that accompany these sometimes volatile companies.

Value funds invest in stocks in public companies that are undervalued. The stocks in the fund may have fallen out of favor. Perhaps the company has experienced difficulties but is turning around.

Load funds. One of the more confusing aspects of mutual funds is that many of them charge a "load". Sales loads are commissions paid to brokers and can range from 4 percent to 8.5 percent. Sometimes, salespeople forget to mention these. For instance, if you purchase $1000 in a mutual fund with a 5 percent load, only $950 of your money will be working for you. Some argue that load funds have better fund managers, but this is generally considered untrue. There is no proof that load funds do any better than no-load funds.

No-load funds. Cost-conscious investors can buy no-load funds directly from the fund management companies. Transactions are handled by mail and there is no commission. They will mail you the forms or you can download them on the Internet. The fund management companies offer a variety of services, including toll-free numbers with experienced customer service personnel. And, with a no-load fund, 100 percent of your money begins working for you right away.

However, if you're afraid to go it alone, working with a broker is better than doing nothing at all. In this case, you might

Sheila Peters

consider a load fund if you feel you really need the advice. Hopefully, the fund's annual yield will surpass the commission. As an example: If the sales commission is 6% and your fund increases in value by 10% that year, you would still be ahead of the game. However, you could pay the commission and your mutual fund could drop in value. There are no guarantees. Another reason to use a broker might be to buy special funds. Fidelity has load funds that invest in particular industries like electronics or computers and these can be the hottest performers in the market. But, be aware that the hottest funds can also be the most volatile. WARNING: Bungee jumpers only.

Hidden Fees

I was well into the game before I discovered that I was paying fees for the fund's operating cost. I felt like the baby bear when he discovered Goldilocks had eaten his porridge. Don't ask me who I thought was paying the costs—certainly not me. Fees include paying the fund manager, servicing the toll-free phone lines, printing and mailing the prospectus, and all the customer service, including the knowledgeable woman who answered my questions on the phone. Management expenses can range from .18 percent to over 2 percent. These are deducted before your earnings are calculated so you typically don't see them. Higher expenses mean lower returns to you.

And, if that's not challenging enough, there are also alphabet soup funds. Unlike a bowl of steaming soup on a winter's day, there's nothing warm and fuzzy about these funds. Over the years, as investors have learned about sales loads, mutual fund companies have done a better job of hiding the funds' expenses. These are called alphabet soup funds because they are labeled by the letter A, B, C, or D. Shares with the traditional front-end load are usually sold as Class A shares. Class B, C, and D shares are the classes that can have back-end loads which are commissions taken out if you sell your fund after a certain number of years; typically a back-end load is charged if you sell your fund in less than seven years. There can also be ongoing expenses known as 12b-1 fees. These include marketing and advertising fees. One thing for sure is that a salesperson may never mention expense fees unless you ask. And, the only way to be sure that a fund is truly no-load and has no unknown fees is to read the prospectus.

A prospectus is about the dullest reading material in the world. They make backs of cereal boxes look fascinating. But, I sat down with a highlighter and discovered that the prospectus includes the fund's investment objectives, costs, and performance history. The most important information is summarized in the first few pages. I was relieved to learn that none of my funds had a 12b-1 fee, no thanks to my investing acumen. The rest of the financial gobbledy gook was filed away for late night episodes of insomnia.

Fund Choices

Since there are over 10,000 mutual funds available, it's hard to know where to begin. Mary Rowland says that if you can afford only one fund, that's better than leaving it in the bank. In that case, she suggests an index fund which gives broad diversification and has very low expenses. You can invest in a S&P 500 which tracks the 500 largest stocks. If you can buy more than one fund, she recommends starting your mutual fund portfolio with three funds; large cap, small cap, and international. She suggests that you own no more than 12 funds. More than that is hard to manage and you would probably be duplicating your efforts.

One of the best sources of information on mutual funds for consumers is Morningstar, a fund research firm. Their monthly newsletter, *Morningstar Investor*, is about $79 a year and includes information on funds that can help you make investment decisions. (800-876-5005) Morningstar also has a fabulous web site (wwww.morningstar.com) that allows you to see what the funds objectives are, past performance, and management fees. It is also available at most libraries.

Both Fidelity and Vanguard publish newsletters for their mutual fund holders. Of course, these tout their own funds, but the general information is quite helpful. Other good resources for print information on mutual funds are *USA Today*, *The Wall Street Journal*, and *Money Magazine*.

Fidelity (800/544-8888) and Vanguard Group (800-662-7447) are the largest mutual fund companies in America. Fidelity has about 100 branch offices throughout the U.S. and staffs its phones 24 hours a day, 365 days a year. If you get marooned on hold, it's probably me tying up the line. This could be why their expenses tend to be somewhat higher than Vanguard.

The average Vanguard fund has an operating expense ratio of .30 percent. Vanguard funds tend to be more conservative and cost conscious. They were the first to offer index funds and they are still the leader in this category.

You can also buy funds from discount brokers like Charles Schwab (800-5-NO-LOAD). These are like a mutual fund supermarket. They allow you to buy and sell mutual funds from different fund companies, all under one umbrella. One phone call. One monthly statement. One tax statement. However, they do charge a transaction fee. But, these are usually less than the sales commissions that you would pay to buy a load fund.

Before you buy a fund, ask questions, and lots of them. You can get plenty of input, but, ultimately, the decision to buy or not will be solely yours. Asking people for financial help because you're a rookie is ok, but you will eventually need to educate yourself. After all, who knows better than you what you really want and need. I also learned that lesson on my trip to Mexico.

When in Mexico - Lesson #2

A few days after the *uno frio cervesa* episode, my friend and I went into a restaurant in Puerto Vallarta. It was a rather remote location and the waiter shook his head when I raised my eyebrows and said "Englais?" My friend randomly pointed to something on the menu and the waiter nodded. At that very moment, a stray dog poked his head in what would have been the front door had there been one, sniffed the air, and then scampered off. Considering it a forewarning, I drew my best rendition of a chicken. The waiter cocked his head from one side to the other, nodded, took the menu and left. But each time he reappeared, he placed another plate in front of my friend but nothing for me. I patiently sipped my Coke as she ate a three-course meal.

"This is delicious," she said. "Are you sure he understood you?"

"Sure he did," I said. "I ordered chicken." Ten minutes later, he lay the bill on the table, mumbled *Gracias*, and shuffled away.

Admitting your ignorance will only get you so far. If you're traveling to parts unknown, you'll need to learn the language. And, if you're traveling in the world of finance and haven't mastered the basics, there's only one word you'll need in your vocabulary regarding your money—*Adios.*

Sheila Peters

Chapter 6
Buying Stocks

Is an all-women investment club a good place to learn?

> *I don't mind living in a man's world,
> as long as I can be a woman in it.*
> — Marilyn Monroe

I was once the membership coordinator for a tennis club and fielded calls for new recruits. One of my primary functions was to determine their level of play, which, over the telephone, could be a fuzzy conversation. Because we played only doubles, it was important that everyone be, at minimum, an intermediate player. After a year, I noticed a definite gender pattern and could almost predict who would make the cut.

The men who claimed they were naturally athletic and wanted to bypass tryouts had a high rate of washout. They would swagger into the clubhouse in a cloud of testosterone and jog out to the courts. Sometimes they would leap over the net. Strangely enough, from the lobby window I would often see these men hogging the court or ricocheting balls off the walls and ceiling. I once saw a man lob the ball off the back of his partner's head.

Conversely, the female players often underrated their level of play. Surprisingly, many were more consistent and skilled. Of course, you could argue that only the more confident women would even show up for tryouts. But the real difference was that the women were more realistic about their level of play. If they did not make the cut, they would exit through the lobby and ask if they could try out again. I never saw the testosterone men

Sheila Peters

leave. They must have exited through the fire door or hid behind the tarp until we all left.

Would it be any surprise to see these same male athletes as investors, boasting loudly at a party about their latest hot stock? Of course, amnesia would set in when asked if they had bought any dogs. Unfortunately, the testosterone persona surfaces frequently in investing circles. No wonder women choose not to participate. Men, it will come as no surprise, tend to think they know more than they do, ask fewer questions and request help less often. They also tend to act on hot tips rather than solid research and take more hazardous risks. Men are also trained not to let on if they are dumbfounded. Let's be honest. Do you know any women who would drive around for hours rather than pull into a gas station and ask for directions?

According to a *Money Magazine*, women are not only as capable as men of making financial decisions, but superior to them in several ways. Women have been socialized to believe that they cannot compete with men, physically or mentally. Paradoxically, in that weakness lies their strength. Financial experts cite five basic characteristics that women possess that are essential qualities for smart financial decision making.

1. They admit ignorance.
2. They seek help.
3. They avoid risk
4. They do homework
5. They set goals.

Afraid that I would encounter the testosterone syndrome in investing classes, I sat mute against the back wall, fearing that I would ask a stupid question and set women back a century or more. I tried reading books, but in the end, absorbed nothing more than every crumb of food in the house.

When a friend invited me to join her investment club, I hesitated. I didn't want to lock in with a group of people who

You Don't Have to Be a Bag Lady!
A Humorous Survival Guide for the Reluctant Investor

would have control over my investments. After all, the idea of saving money was so that I could be independent. Still, having heard about the success of the Beardstown Ladies, I wanted to know more.

The Berwyn Ladies

It turned out that the group of eight women had been together for two years and got along quite well. Several of them grew up in Berwyn, a suburb outside of Chicago where, after college, I had worked at a JCPenney. It was here that I rented my first apartment and lived for two years. At the time, Berwyn was predominantly immigrant or first generation Polish, German, and Czechoslovakian. Like much of Chicago, the streets were lined with rows of no-nonsense yellow and red brick bungalows with sturdy concrete steps. The houses were set so close together, you could almost reach out your fork and taste the pirogi on your neighbor's dinner plate. So close, in fact, sometimes a husband tried to coax his key into the wrong front door in the wee hours of the night after a few too many brewskis. I know that's true, because it happened to me. The police had to pry a persistent man off my porch at 2 a.m., but only after I insisted, through the mail slot of my chained and double-bolted door that, no, I *really* wasn't missing a husband. As it turns out, he lived ten houses down. But, overall, Berwyn was a clean safe neighborhood.

Each morning at JCPenney, I opened the doors and stepped out of the way for babushka-clad old ladies wearing drab woolen coats. They would trudge from the bus stop pulling their wheeled carts. On Saturdays, they brought their husbands instead. They laid cash on the counter for everything, especially large purchases like refrigerators, stoves and washing machines. Like many survivors of the depression, they didn't trust banks. I thought they were funny. Funny until I learned that many of them amassed small fortunes in either apartment buildings or in their mattresses. Oftentimes, both.

Twenty years later, I found myself sitting in a Berwyn bungalow, talking with eight ladies about investing. But, something was different. The furniture and lampshades weren't covered with the original factory plastic. In the Berwyn I had known, those from the old country preserved their first floors for company, but watched TV and had a complete kitchen in the basement. Had I come so far up in the world that I was now invited into the parlor? Probably not. Unlike their parents, this generation was less steeped in deferred gratification. Mind you, I did spot a few doilies; but, that didn't fool me. Upstairs, downstairs, plastic, no plastic, these women were still the daughters of Berwyn. My money would not have been safer in Fort Knox.

After bumbling along by myself for so long, it was refreshing to meet women who were serious about investing and shared my desire to learn. Best of all, I would feel comfortable asking questions, even stupid questions. I quickly scribbled out a check before they could vote me out.

Mutual Support and Gain

I learned that investment clubs have been around since 1900. The Mutual Investment Club of Detroit started in 1951 with $800. Today, it's worth over $4 million—not including the $1.2 million in withdrawals that members have already taken. The actual amount invested was $400,000. Not bad for a group of people who probably started out not knowing price earnings ratio from earnings per share. But over time, together, they learned. They pooled their resources—experience, money and research—and built a nest egg for the future. *A Faberge egg.*

Investment clubs have tripled since 1993. Today there are over 30,000 clubs. The longest running bull market in history is why. Since WWII, the stock market has averaged a 10% return.

With paltry CD returns of 5% and 6%, people are joining clubs in droves to learn about investing, have some fun, and start growing their own nest eggs. The average age of most clubs reporting is 6-7 years.

The ladies assured me that I would learn how to gather information, read and analyze financial reports, and select individual stocks to buy. They also said that I would learn how to track stocks and decide when the time was right to buy, hold or sell. If I had any remaining doubts, when they served coffee and strawberry shortcake, I knew I was in the right place. I made a mental note to plot out all the Polish bakeries on the way home.

Like most clubs, ours is a member of NAIC, National Association of Investors Corporation, which was founded in 1951. It is a non-profit organization and the leading authority on starting and running a successful investment club. Their primary purpose is to help clubs and individuals become more successful investors by providing educational materials. They show investors how to invest in companies that are growing more rapidly than the economy. They help investors evaluate whether the stock price is reasonable in relation to future profits. NAIC has 4 fundamental rules:

1. Invest regularly over a long period of time.
2. Reinvest earnings as they are received.
3. Learn how to pick companies that are growing.
4. Diversify

Stocks Come in all Sizes

Just as with mutual funds, stocks can be categorized. To understand their differences, I referred to *Investing for Dummies*, by Eric Tyson. I learned that the size of a company is defined by the total market value of its outstanding stock, called its capitalization. So, if there are 1 million shares sold and each share is $5, the total market value is $5 million. Small companies have total market values—small capitalization—of less than $1 billion. Medium-sized companies have market values between $1 billion and $5 billion. Large-capitalization companies have market values greater than $5 billion.

Growth stocks are public companies that are growing much faster than the economy. As long as earnings keep growing at or above the analysts' predictions, the stocks' prices will continue to rise. But if they miss their earnings targets, and sometimes by only a fraction, prices can plummet quickly. These stocks are for gutsy people who are willing to pay a higher price because they believe the stock will appreciate rapidly. Technology companies are in this category. These are for bungee jumpers. Up...Down. Up...Down. Sometimes, however, what goes down never comes back up.

Value stocks tend to be public companies whose products or services will always be in demand. The stock price may be cheap, or at least reasonable, compared to the company's assets and potential profits. Bargain hunters hope to pick up stocks that may have fallen out of favor. The hope is not so much that the stock prices will have explosive growth, but that they will return to a fair market value. Value stocks are usually less volatile than growth stocks and tend to be popular when investors become less aggressive and more defensive.

Invest in Knowledge First

With over 36,000 stocks in the U.S. alone, it's hard to know where to begin. Employing Peter Lynch of Fidelity's "know-what-you-own" approach, I began by researching JC Penney. After all, I had worked there for 6 years and thought they were a good company. I also researched their competition: Wal-Mart and Target. I have always felt more comfortable using the "rule of 3" in comparing products, whether it's for car insurance, linoleum or a handyman.

You Don't Have to Be a Bag Lady!
A Humorous Survival Guide for the Reluctant Investor

I began with the Value Line Investment Survey, which is the bible of investment researching. The report costs about $600 per year to subscribe, but is available at your local library to make copies. At first glance, this report is intimidating to even a Certified Public Accountant. The print is so small I had to use a magnifying ruler. With the help of *Terry Savage Talks Money*, I was better able to understand Value Line which condenses down to a single page the key information and statistics about a stock and the company behind the stock. It gives information on performance, sales, profits, earnings, and the future outlook. It also shows the price earnings ratio which can be a tip-off that the stock is overvalued.

I entered the figures from Value Line into the Stock Selection Guide (SSG), an analysis tool available through NAIC. This program is available to both members and nonmembers of NAIC and can be done manually or with the help of a computer program. NAIC also offers classes at libraries, community centers and community colleges on how to work with this report. Quite honestly, the hardest part is reading the small print on Value Line and picking up the figures correctly.

The SSG helps you analyze historical data along with your projections about the future of the company. The program can not tell you whether you should buy or sell a stock, but it can help confirm how favorably you feel about the future of the company. I also looked up articles about the retailers on the Internet. I learned that Wal-Mart planned to expand aggressively, especially in foreign markets. The club was eager to hear the results of my research.

Sheila Peters

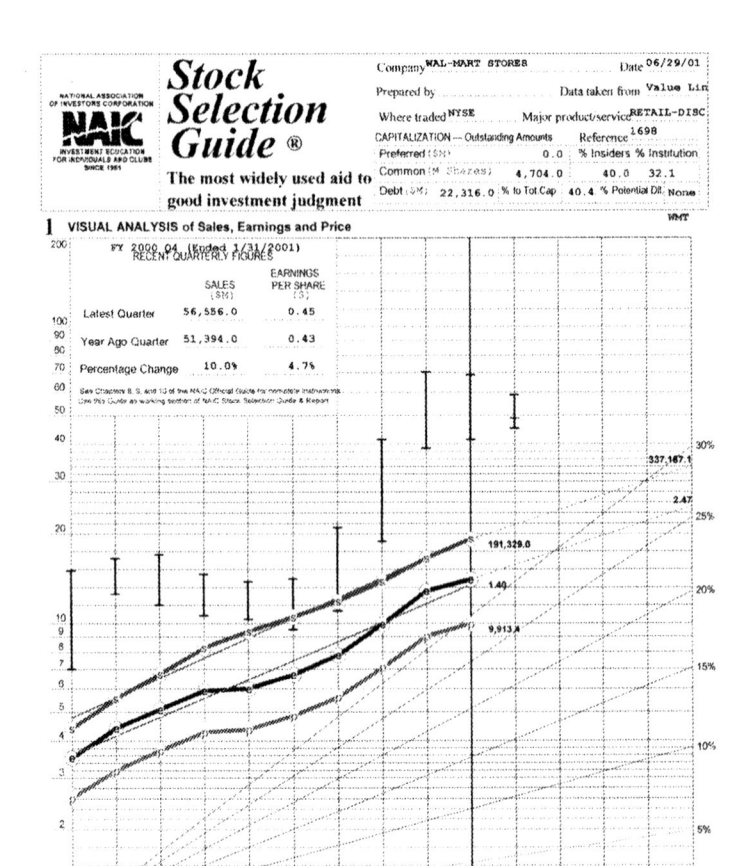

Stock Selection Guide ®

The most widely used aid to good investment judgment

NATIONAL ASSOCIATION OF INVESTORS CORPORATION — NAIC — INVESTMENT EDUCATION FOR INDIVIDUALS AND CLUBS SINCE 1951

Company	WAL-MART STORES
Date	06/29/01
Prepared by	
Data taken from	Value Line
Where traded	NYSE
Major product/service	RETAIL-DISC
CAPITALIZATION — Outstanding Amounts	Reference 1698
Preferred ($M)	0.0
% Insiders	40.0
% Institution	32.1
Common (M Shares)	4,704.0
Debt ($M)	22,316.0
% to Tot Cap	40.4
% Potential Dil.	None

1 VISUAL ANALYSIS of Sales, Earnings and Price

FY 2000_04 (Ended 1/31/2001)

RECENT QUARTERLY FIGURES

	SALES ($M)	EARNINGS PER SHARE ($)
Latest Quarter	56,556.0	0.45
Year Ago Quarter	51,394.0	0.43
Percentage Change	10.0%	4.7%

See Chapters 8, 9, and 10 of the NAIC Official Guide for complete instructions. Use this Guide as working section of NAIC Stock Selection Guide & Report.

337,187.1
2.47
191,329.0
1.40
9,913.4

(1) Historical Sales Growth .... 16.8 %
(2) Estimated Future Sales Growth ... 12.0 %
(3) Historical Earnings Per Share Growth .... 15.8 %
(4) Estimated Future Earnings Per Share Growth ... 12.0 %

Printed: 06/29/01 05:29 PM Prepared by: Using The NAIC Investor's Toolkit

You Don't Have to Be a Bag Lady!
A Humorous Survival Guide for the Reluctant Investor

This material is copyrighted and taken from The Official Guide from The National Association of Investors Corporation Starting and Running a Profitable Investment Club.

Sheila Peters

Price Earnings Ratio

First, we reviewed the financial information entered into the Stock Selection Guide. This report converts the financial information into a graph that conveys a strong visual message about the company's growth in sales, earnings and profits. We also looked at the price earnings ratio (P/E ratio), which is the current stock price per share divided by the annual earnings per share. This measure helps determine if a stock is priced too high. For instance, if Wal-Mart's stock price is $50 and their annual earnings per share is $2, the P/E ratio would be 25 (50 divided by 2 equals 25). If JCPenney's stock price is $50, but their annual earnings per share is $1, the P/E ratio is 50 (50 divided by 1 equals 50). The difference in P/E ratio tells me that Wal-Mart stock is a better value because for every $50 share of stock, the earnings would be $2. Each share of JCPenney stock would yield half, or only $1. Comparing stocks within the same industry, a lower P/E ratio will indicate that there is more profit per dollar.

To help understand why different industries have varying ranges of P/E ratios, think of the price-per-pound of meat in the grocery store. There might be three grades of ground beef ranging from $.99 to $1.69 per pound. You would determine the best value by considering content and freshness. Conversely, filet mignon would cost quite a bit more per pound, so you would not compare it to the price of ground beef. If you did spot filet mignon at $1.69, you probably wouldn't buy it, suspecting there was something wrong. In the same way, you wouldn't compare P/E ratios of companies in different industries. The average P/E ratios for different industries appears on the industry summary pages for Value Line.

Some investors were not deterred by high P/E ratios especially in the high tech industry. Many of the Internet companies had no earnings at all. Stockholders were speculating that the companies would grow and the gains would primarily come from the stock prices going up. However, over the long term, companies cannot survive without earnings. When the tech bubble burst, there was only one way for the stocks to go—down. Tech investors paid filet mignon prices for what turned out to be White Castle burgers. Sadder but wiser investors have learned that if price races too far ahead of earnings, the stock is probably over valued.

Personal Experience Counts

After my report on retail companies, we began discussing the pros and cons of each stock. We talked about our personal shopping experiences. Would we go back to shop at the store? Did the company have future potential? Was it a growing industry? Because our club meeting was a safe and supportive environment, everyone felt free to express her opinion.

Typically, women are savvy shoppers when it comes to comparing price and quality on clothes, groceries, and the whole range of consumer products. But, they can't imagine buying an intangible like stocks or mutual funds. Nevertheless, many of the same principles apply. We eat fast foods at McDonalds and Burger King, fly United or Southwest, use AT&T or MCI. Most of us have computers and use the Internet. We are consumers and our collective buying power determines whether a company will grow or not.

According to a *Money Magazine* article, Thomas O'Hara, one of the founders of NAIC, claimed that his club posted annual losses for more than 20 years. That was until the former all-male club, composed of 18 former Wayne State fraternity brothers, decided to let their wives join the group. Within four years, the club's stock value tripled, taking it from $180,000 in 1982 to $500,000 in 1985. "Things just turned right around once the women started picking stocks," said O'Hara.

NAIC statistics from 1981 through 1996 show that women-only investing clubs earned a 21.3% average annual return while men-only clubs earned a 15% average annual return. Those results strongly suggest that a significant number of women have mastered effective investing. They have proved themselves to be not only as capable as men, but often superior to them in several ways. Only recently are men's clubs closing the gap.

In our investment club, if we are interested in buying a stock, a majority of the members must vote for the purchase and the purchase price. Studies have shown that women, more than men, are comfortable in an atmosphere of consensus. No one person dominates the decision-making. This creates an atmosphere of co-operation, not competition.

Market or Limit Orders

There are two ways to buy. A market order is executed when a stock is purchased at the current market price. A limit order is executed when a stock is bought at a stated price, purchasing it only if it drops to or below that number. The broker holds the order for a set time or until our asking price matches the market. We generally spend $1,000 to $1500, so we buy the number of shares available for that amount. We collectively decided that since Wal-Mart's stock price was at its 52-week high, we would consider a buy if it dropped 5 points. Since stock prices can fluctuate daily, we decided to stuff the money under the club mattress and wait for a dip. Sometimes it works, sometimes it doesn't. We look for stocks that have growth potential and hold onto them. No day traders in this bunch. Trading too frequently can result in transaction fees eating up all your gains.

The Club Advantage

One of the nice things about a club is that you benefit from several people researching stocks. Chances are, someone in your club will work in the industry you are researching and can share valuable insights. How does the industry view the company?

Do they pay their bills on time? Experienced clubs will not just analyze one stock; they will also look at the competition. And, if the club decides to pass on the stock, you still may like it enough to buy it yourself. You can place a buy through your club broker or set up an on-line account yourself. Over time, you can build your own stock portfolio. To learn more about NAIC and their local chapters, refer to their Web site: www.better-investing.org.

If you decide to join an existing club, go to a few of their meetings and see if your goals are compatible. If it is not for you, don't be discouraged; you can always start your own club. This gives you the advantage of starting out fresh with people who are at your same investment level. Many clubs start out with a common bond: co-workers, neighbors, friends, and family. After all, you're not going to forge a long term relationship with people you have nothing in common with except making money. Clubs can also be a rewarding social outlet.

There are plenty of books on starting your own club. *The Beardstown Ladies' Common Sense Investment Guide* is a popular book that has fueled investment-club fever. In addition, you might want to pick up *Starting and Running a Profitable Investment Club: The Official Guide From the NAIC,* by Thomas O'Hara.

To start, make a list of 15 people you feel would be compatible. You will need it big enough to spread out the work. Invite them to meet and talk about their investment goals, risk levels, and ideas about the market. Make it a potluck and have some fun. Most clubs are comfortable with 10-15 people. In considering members, choose people who enjoy each other's company. Members should agree on an investment philosophy. All members should be prepared to investigate and analyze securities and make periodic reports. Some clubs have initial costs for computer software and educational materials. Members typically invest $25 to $50 a month. That, of course, is in addition to the cost for desserts, which in any respectable club should be the first order of business.

Making money isn't the only benefit to joining a club. For me, almost as rewarding was a man's surprised nod of agreement a few years ago (before the tech wreck) when I said, "Microsoft? Sure, I know it's split three times since 1996, but don't you think those P/E ratios are kind of in the nosebleed section?"

You Don't Have to Be a Bag Lady!
A Humorous Survival Guide for the Reluctant Investor

Chapter 7
Researching on the Internet

Can the Internet make you rich?

> *Trust no one with your money. Because no one is smarter than you when it comes to your money. Well, they may be smarter, but you care more.*
> —Joan Rivers

According to *USA Today*, more than 40% of Americans use the Internet at home—up from 27% in 1998. This translates to almost 40 million users in 1999. More and more, it's enabling people to do their shopping from home. However, most people claim that their primary reason for going online is to research or get information. Until recently, I belonged to the 60% of nonusers who either didn't see the benefits of the Internet, were secretly intimidated by it, or were too cheap to pay the monthly fee. Guilty on all three counts.

In my defense, I had tried AOL several years ago, but found it painfully slow. What I remember most was hunching over the screen, downloading information. By the time the site flashed on, I'd forgotten what I was waiting for. I found the Internet hard to navigate, which it was originally, and deduced that people were using it for e-mail or chat rooms - a cyber variation of a local bar at 2 am. People with nothing worthwhile to say and all night to do it.

To be honest, I have never been a trailblazer in the world of technology. Other than my mother, I was probably the last person east of the Mississippi to hook up an answering machine. I was convinced that if I had the Internet, I would never use it.

Sheila Peters

Why waste the money? My friends think I'm cheap, but they don't know the half of it. My real problem is that I had heard, "We can't afford that," for so many years, it was seared into my hard drive. By the time I was an adult and had my own money, it became "Do you really need that?" My computer, which had served me well as a word processor, was too slow to bother installing the Internet. And therein lay my dilemma; I couldn't justify buying a new computer simply to fiddle around in cyberspace. In our family, it was a sin to throw out anything that still worked. And, oddly enough, especially when it had a plug. There was a special room in hell for those who wasted.

It wasn't that our family was poor. There was enough money to keep the wolf from the door, but, according to my mother, the beast was never far away. I never heard of "seconds" until I ate dinner at a friend's house. At home, we just stopped eating when the food on our plate was gone. Seconds were what my mother stashed away for the second night. We would watch with crinkled noses as she ran the previous night's mashed potatoes and hamburgers through a food grinder, slap them into patties and drop them into a greased iron skillet. To this day, when I spot bananas cut in half, I see my father slicing them in the kitchen. "Children waste," he'd say. My mother often spoke of "modest servings". We were learning to stretch our resources.

But, I couldn't stretch my resources to include a new computer and maintain a clear conscience. When I learned that I could access my Fidelity account online, I headed to the library. The librarian directed me to a dog-eared sign up sheet. After my allotted thirty minutes I got kicked off. I sheepishly spied on ten-year-olds as they clicked away with the same ease as they skateboarded. Fearing extinction, I signed up for an Internet class at the local college.

I quickly learned the first rule about adult education computer classes; never let on that you "get it". After the first hour, it was evident that many of the students were in worse shape than I was. Like shipwrecked passengers, they grabbed at anyone clinging to a scrap of information. By week two, I began muttering in a low tone, "This stupid thing doesn't work." They dismissed me as useless and rushed off to their next victim. By week three there were only a handful of us left. I learned how to pull up the Fidelity and Yahoo sites. With a sense of mastery, I bookmarked my favorite pages. Half of what the teacher said sailed right over my head, but I didn't care. I was out of park and cruising down Wall Street.

Navigating the Internet

The most rewarding aspect of the Internet is the speedy access to information. In the old days, if you wanted a fund prospectus, you had to call the fund company and have it mailed. Today, you can log onto the fund company's web site and view the prospectus immediately. Information on the Internet is often up-to-the-minute. Large companies have entire staffs responsible for keeping their sites current.

Now that I was hooked, I couldn't bear waiting my turn at the library. I shamefully thought about whiting out names on the sign up sheet. My mind flashed back to corn-on-the-cob night at our house. It was one of our many character-building events because we owned only six corn skewers. If you were quick on the draw, you grabbed one skewer and poked your fork on the other end. Taking two was a declaration of war. The losers either waited for the others to finish their corn or improvised with paper towels and any sharp object they could find. My parents must have deliriously believed that we would learn to share. What we learned was to move fast and deal with the consequences later.

These were my first awarenesses that we lived in a world of scarcity. There would never be enough chairs, forks, car window seats, bathrooms, parents' attention, and on infinitum. And it goes without saying; there would never be enough money.

Sheila Peters

But when I clicked on the Internet, I stepped into a world of abundance, with more financial sites than you can shake a mouse at. Tons. The information is endless and overwhelming. And the best part was that, for once, someone couldn't get there before me and empty it out. I flitted from site to site and soon realized that I was lost.

Where to go First

Terry Savage, author of *The Savage Truth on Money*, suggests that when you're just starting out, log onto the Mutual Fund Education Alliance, www.mfea.com. She claims that this web site of the nonprofit, no-load mutual fund association is the broadest and easiest site to use. It has profiles of more than 9,000 no-load funds and an easy search system you can use to select funds that meet your criteria. The site includes an education center which is a wonderful reference. You will also find the latest news about no-load mutual funds. However, this site does not analyze the funds it features.

For that you can go to Morningstar's site, www.morningstar.com. Morningstar is a fund research firm and is one of the better mutual fund web resources. The site features individual mutual funds and shows long term fund performance data and graphs, risk ratings, manager profiles, and information on fees. It also lists discount brokers who sell the fund. You can also read articles on developments in the fund industry. Much of the information is free, but for in-depth analysis, you will have to subscribe. Staying with a few favorite sites and thoroughly exploring them kept me focused.

Most fund companies have their own sites like www.vanguard.com, www.schwab.com, and www.fidelity.com. There is no fee or commission to buy a mutual fund online from the fund company as long as it is one of their funds. They will also sell you stocks with fees ranging from $15-$30. You can access your portfolio 24 hours a day and submit trades when the rest of the world is snoring. Many sites provide online research and analysis. Most sites are becoming more user friendly and feature news, chat rooms, articles and other services designed to help you make intelligent investing decisions. However, don't be lured into thinking that "chat room" and "intelligent" are remotely related.

Getting Serious

On one particular evening when I went into the library, I found the sign-up sheet filled for the entire week. I held my breath for fear I would explode. A lifetime of waiting my turn, just to be turned away, was crushing in on me. Like Scarlet O'Hara raising her clenched fist to the heavens, swearing that she would never go hungry again, I too swore that, "With God as my witness, I would never wait for a computer again." The next day I made my purchase, and in doing so, wheeled my old 386 into the spare bedroom knowing that we would meet up again in hell. Perhaps by then I could fabricate a good defense. I hooked up the Internet and went for a test drive. Time to get serious.

My first obstacle was determining what was advertising and what was legitimate and objective information. In *Mutual Funds For Dummies*, author Eric Tyson warns that investors need to recognize who is paying for the financial site. More often than not, it's a company that's trying to sell you something. Internet sites are primarily funded by the marketing departments of companies. He suggests that you begin by checking out the fine print. If the web page has a button that says something like "About Us", click it. Sometimes you can get information on who's sponsoring the site. Many Internet sites are interactive and you can use their retirement planning calculators and plug in your answers. But, those don't come without strings attached. The site might be releasing your information to marketing companies that now have the lowdown on you.

Sheila Peters

If you decide to buy mutual funds or stocks online and need to find a brokerage firm, Terry Savage suggests looking at Gomez Advisors www.gomez.com. This service rates more than 100 online brokerage firms in terms of price and service. If price is your concern, you will discover brokerage firms that have transaction fees as low as $5. If your goal is to research stocks, one of the benefits to using an online broker is getting reports like the Standard & Poor Stock Report which lists in depth information such as a company's history, earnings, and future outlook. Also helpful is Zack's Investment Research which includes analysts recommendations. However, when buying stocks, it is still a good idea to trot to the library for a copy of Value Line which is not available online for free.

Buying Online can be Deceivingly Simple

One of the negatives about buying funds or stocks on the Internet is that it is just too darned easy. Previously, I had to pick up the telephone and place an order with a broker. It usually took a bit of steam on my part just to make the call. But with one click, I could now own the stock. It was a powerful, but misleading feeling—as if the clicking itself were the work and not the hours of research, not to mention the weekend cooling off, preventing me from buying too impulsively.

I could never understand people who got all revved up in casinos. Despite the constant bells and clangs, I can step onto a riverboat and park myself at a slot machine until my one roll of quarters is depleted. I confess to liking Blackjack, but have never felt that bungee-jumping exhilaration. At least not until I bought my first stock online.

To leap from an even higher bridge, I installed a screensaver program with a stock ticker tape running across the bottom of the computer screen. I plugged in my stocks and watched the prices fluctuate by the hour. Sometimes by the minute. When the numbers glowed red, I chose not to panic, calmly remembering that investing was for the long term. But when the black numbers ran up quickly, my adrenaline raced as I contemplated buying more. Missing out was almost worse than losing. I didn't yet know that markets typically fall faster than they rise. With only a shred of common sense remaining, I removed the program and put the price fluctuations out of my mind…well, almost.

It's hard to listen to the outrageous success stories and not think it's easy to get rich. Day traders buy and sell many times during the day as stocks bounce up and down, taking the profits and losses along the way. However, you usually hear only the success stores. You don't hear about the people who have blown all their retirement money and the second mortgage. According to the Securities and Exchange Commission, 77% of day traders will lose some or all of their money. A *USA Today* article reported that an investigator found that in the Los Angeles office of Providential Securities, not a single client made money, while the average customer lost $50,000. Timing the market is a game that even the professionals can't master.

Most of them will tell you it's not *timing* the market, but time *in* the market that matters.

There's another word of warning when buying investments online. Despite all the advantages technology has to offer, it can't tell you which stocks to buy. You alone are the one who will ultimately make a wise financial choice. Remember, no one will care as much about your investments as you. No one will have as much to lose as you. Use whatever information and help you can get on the Internet as nothing more than a basis for further investigation and discussion. Jeff Wurio, author of *Got Money? Enjoy it! Manage it!,* explains that technology isn't a panacea and nowhere might that hold greater truth than in our financial lives. He also warns that the anonymity of the Internet makes it easy to pretend to be someone you're not. Beware before trusting advice on message boards and chat rooms.

But overall, the good really does outweigh the bad. The Internet has changed the way people invest. Prices for trading stocks has come down and costs will continue to drop as middlemen are squeezed out. Individual investors now have access to the best resources and are more empowered than ever. In the future, information will be a commodity, and people will pay a premium for reliable data and analysis. The market will continue to move smarter, better, and faster. In the next five years, one in five American households, or 14 million people, will have an online investment account.

Overcoming Scarcity

I looked back over the previous six months and marveled at how much I had learned. And there was still so much more. I shook my head remembering how I had felt guilty buying the computer. Always that scarcity thing. I thought back to a day when Angela, Mom and I went on a boat ride. As usual, we were the first people in line to get our tickets. And, of course, we were an hour early. They weren't boarding yet, so we walked down the pier and watched from a distance. Thirty minutes later, Angela leaped up and said, "They're boarding. Hurry up or we won't get a good seat!" We charged down the pier, almost tearing my mother's arms off. After we victoriously settled on the bench, I let out a sigh and looked around. Although the boat held 150 passengers, there were only about twenty on board. I realized that alone I was bad, but together my sister and I were pathetic.

Yes, the meek would inherit the earth, but from early childhood, my sister and I were determined to get our share of the pie. At least in this lifetime. However, in our determination, we didn't realize that an obsession was taking shape. And, as in most childhood defenses, long after we'd outgrown the need, we wouldn't know how to let go of the behavior.

I deduced that it was in our genes and felt vindicated as I counted down in birth order. The boys also carried the fear of scarcity. Obviously, a family malaise. However, I hit a speed bump when I came to Marianne, the last in line. If she didn't look so much like us, I'd have thought my parents brought home the wrong baby. She spent money like water and scoffed at our thriftiness. "You're all so cheap!" I dismissed her criticism, attributing it to her birth order status. As the baby, it's a good bet she never lay awake at night thinking about corn holders.

But I knew that Moira, the second youngest, was no hospital switch. I remember the day she confessed to me after eating at an expensive restaurant with her husband, "Seems like a waste to spend all that money on one meal when I'm just going to be hungry again tomorrow." I nodded in sympathy. Yes, she was one of us. I think her computer is even older than mine.

Sheila Peters

Chapter 8
Hiring Financial Professionals

Why not do it yourself?

> *Only the little people pay taxes.*
> — Leona Helmsley

I never thought to hire someone to manage my finances. After all, the idea was to keep it, not give it away. And besides, I was raised in a do-it-yourself family. What you couldn't do, you did without. On weekends we'd trail behind my father to the hardware store, taking one last breath outside the door and holding our noses to the myriad of paint smells. The pitted hardwood floor was strewn with paint cans, odd shaped pipes and coils of wire, weaving a labyrinth to the service counter in the back. The store was usually empty except for the owner, hunched over some contraption and poking at it with a screwdriver. Behind him were shelves filled with broken toasters, lamps and radios. Dad never bought more than a handful of nuts and bolts; he just wanted to swap fix-it stories with the owner. It was hardware heaven. My father spent nights in his workshop tinkering. After all, it was in his genes.

During the depression, as the story goes, my grandfather invented and patented a non-jamming component for the three-cherry slot machine and my grandmother peddled it. So there was always this expectation that the inventor gene would surface again in somebody. But, it would be a long wait. Once, Dad built a grandfather clock from spare parts. I watched him unscrew the motor from the old washing machine and transplant it into the clock. He carved the hands from a slat of venetian blind. The tic-tock was so loud, someone usually crept down at

Sheila Peters

night to turn it off. Thirty years later it's still lulling my mother to sleep at night.

Naturally, when I bought my first home, I did all the repairs. Having watched my father and brothers do it for years, I didn't hesitate to lay tiles, replace electrical fixtures, and even put in a sump pump. I spent a lot of time in hardware stores, and still holding my nose. It never occurred to me to hire someone to fix anything. So hiring a professional to manage my money was even more outlandish. Anyhow, there was nothing to manage, only scrape together.

Good Reasons to Hire a Professional

Most women feel the same. No matter what size their portfolio, they never think it is substantial enough to warrant hiring a financial professional. What I didn't realize, though, is that making money is only half of the equation. Keeping it from Uncle Sam can be almost as challenging. That may be one reason why you want to hire a financial professional. Hiring someone doesn't mean you've thrown in the towel; it means you're smart enough to get support in the areas where you lack experience in making decisions. Because there is so much to know about money management, unless it is your full time job, chances are you'd be better off hiring a professional. Just as a plumber can save money by fixing pipes before leaks cause major damage, so can an advisor help clean up money problems before they become major. You don't have to do it all by yourself.

As I talked with people about finance, I learned that there are many different services that financial professionals can provide. You can hire a financial planner, a money manager or a broker.

You Don't Have to Be a Bag Lady!
A Humorous Survival Guide for the Reluctant Investor

Financial Planner

A financial planner is a person trained to advise you on a broad range of financial subjects and is paid for in various ways. She will help you analyze your financial situation, set up a program to help you meet your objectives and keep you on track. It's like having a financial coach.

Financial planners can help you make decisions about your 401K, IRA's and Roth IRA's. They can also educate you on the tax consequences of selling your investments. For instance, if you sell shares of stock, you will owe taxes on any profit over your original cost or get a deduction from a loss. *When* you sell is within your control. That's not the case with mutual funds, which are made up of stocks of several companies and are bought and sold during the year by the fund manager to get the best return. These transactions will result in capital gains every year. You will need to report these gains on your income tax forms. If you want more control over those taxes, your financial planner can advise you of funds that have a minimum number of transactions or steer you to other investments.

Planners are paid in one of three ways.

- *Fee only.* They sell only advice.
- *Commission only.* Their services are free, but they are paid a commission on products they sell you like mutual funds, stocks and bonds.
- *Fee plus commission.* They charge an up-front fee for advice and then charge commission on the financial products they sell.

Finding a Financial Planner

One way to find a financial advisor is by word of mouth, but you are strongly advised not to use a friend. The planner who meets your needs today might not tomorrow. Mixing business and pleasure makes it difficult to fire your planner. Also, beware of media personalities who are selling investments. In all likelihood, they're not certified financial planners. They're just talking heads.

There are a lot of people hanging out their shingle, claiming to be financial planners. Many of them moonlight and have no more under their belt than a weekend course and a certificate. Many of the special funds they sell you are similar to those you can buy directly from a fund company. The difference is that the fund companies don't charge a commission. To make it worse, there's not a lot of regulation in the industry. If you decide to meet a financial planner, do background checks. Look for professionals with the initials CFP (Certified Financial Planner).

Use credentials as a starting point, but not the only deciding factor. Credentials are a sign that someone is proficient in the number crunching side of financial planning but knowledge alone does not make a good planner. Service and manner make the difference in a successful relationship. Follow your gut. No matter how well recommended the advisor is, you need to check her out. Even if you're smart enough not to pick a scoundrel, you might not spot a planner who just isn't very good for you.

Here are a few sample questions to ask an analyst.

- What is your educational and professional background?
- How do you get paid?
- What services will I get for the commission I pay?
- How often will I hear from you?
- Will anyone else be working with me?

Money Managers

Some of my friends have hired money managers to oversee their investments. Money managers often make the investment decisions and execute the trades. They are usually paid as a percentage of assets managed. Fees can range from 1% to 3%.

They normally only work with investors who have at least $100,000 to invest. Not only didn't I have that kind of money, I wasn't sure I'd feel comfortable giving someone that much control. Money managers are fine for some investors, but it can be easy for some women to confuse their financial planner with Prince Charming. They think they have finally found someone to take care of them. But remember—no one will ever care as much about your money as you. And, no one will ever have as much to lose as you.

Brokers

Some investors work with a full-service broker, someone licensed to sell individual stocks and bonds and paid by commission. They handle all transactions and identify investment opportunities for their clients. They are not financial planners; their primary job is to sell securities. If you are willing to do your own research on stocks, you can use a discount broker who provides no information, only does the transaction. Discount brokers are paid a salary. You alone will decide which service you want to work with. If you are a buy and hold investor, price is less important than getting the service that you want. Some people hire a full service broker for advice and research but use a discounter when they come up with their own ideas. It is more important to do business where you feel comfortable and people take the time to service your account properly than to save a few dollars on the trade.

The Art of Jerry-Rigging

I found the choices so confusing, like many women, I did nothing. I figured I knew enough to get by. Just like my do-it-yourself gene was getting me by with home repairs. But, as the years went by, it was clear that I was better at some things than others. For instance, there were those loose floor tiles in the kitchen and the curling wall paper in the bathroom. And the pail

Sheila Peters

under the kitchen sink. From watching my father work, I learned discipline and perseverance. But my brothers taught me the art of jerry-rigging.

After my father died, the house slowly headed south. Over time, broomsticks propped open windows where latch hooks had long since broken off. A pair of pliers rested on the TV stand to change channels. Two jacks were braced under the back porch to keep it from falling off. If the house repairs were creative, our cars were even more so. My younger brothers, who had more of the inventor gene, tore cars apart and rebuilt them into cars that still didn't run. Uncoiled hangers replaced missing antennas. Rope secured trunks that refused to stay shut. Once, they put a radio in my car, but installed it inside the glove compartment.

And just parking all those junkers took a fair amount of creativity. With eight kids, we had almost as many cars. We bickered constantly about the garage because no one wanted to park inside it. That's because the barn-like doors slid open on overhead rollers and derailed every time someone honked. I can still see my mother in her red Sunday coat raising a pitchfork to coax the rollers back on.

My younger brother solved the problem the day he burned down the garage. Mark was the one who held the most inventor potential, but was also the one shuffling around sheepishly whenever there were blackouts and explosions. The demise of the garage might have been considered a blessing were it not for the motorcycle and two cars that charbroiled inside. However, when the debris was cleared away, we all agreed that we could fit in more cars if the garage wasn't rebuilt. Mom always says everything works out for the best.

Jerry-Rigged Investing

My investments were jerry-rigged too—an annuity, a money market account, a stock mutual fund—all held together with no overall financial plan. I had talked to different people but didn't

You Don't Have to Be a Bag Lady!
A Humorous Survival Guide for the Reluctant Investor

really work with any one person. Charles Jaffe, author of *The Right Way to Hire Financial Help*, explains that most people take advice from one advisor, move on to another and another without establishing a cohesive plan. Ricocheting among advisors leads to short term thinking and a hodgepodge of holdings, creating mistakes.

Sensing rising water, I responded to a local bank's ad for financial planning. I sat down in a corner office with a man in a blue suit and tie. He spoke authoritatively so I felt that I had come to the right place. We talked for about five minutes when he said, "Is your husband coming?"

"I'm not married," I responded, not understanding the relevance.

"Oh," he said and then began talking about different investment opportunities which were all new to me. I asked questions and took notes. I was determined to do this the right way. However, as time wore on, his answers became shorter and more vague. I was waiting for him to ask me how much money I was investing, but he never did. After twenty minutes, he suggested that I think about the investments and we'd meet again in a few weeks. Sounded good to me.

When I returned, he wasn't there. His secretary's eyes avoided mine as she explained that my name was nowhere on his calendar. Yes, she would have him call me. Heat prickled up my back and neck as I left the lobby. By the time I pulled out of the parking lot, my face was burning. I didn't bother calling him back. Instead, I took my $25,000 to Fidelity and invested in mutual funds.

Actually, this man did me more good than harm. And I wasn't wrong to ask all those questions. The rule of thumb in financial relationships is very simple: ***Never do anything you don't understand.*** And, choose a planner who wants to hire you as much as you want to hire them.

Sheila Peters

Short Cuts Don't Pay

Around that time, I was immersed in another of my do-it-yourself projects—spray painting my green refrigerator to a more contemporary white. I considered it a brilliant way to save money until I had already applied three cans of paint. The refrigerator sat in the middle of the kitchen with plastic drop cloths draped around it like an emergency room. The front was a mass of white dribbles and clumps. The top was streaked and the side was bubbled. There was more paint on me and the tarp than on the refrigerator. The plastic stuck to my shoes as I stepped around; I was like a bug stuck in fly paper. But, I had bigger problems—I was out of paint. The fine print on the can read: *apply additional coats within one hour or wait 24 hours.* I couldn't go to the store covered in paint or live with the plastic getup one more day. I let the refrigerator dry and shoved it back into it's nook. Fortunately, the green sides were against the side and back walls. I realized that with the amount of time and energy I had spent on the refrigerator, I could have gotten a part time job at Taco Bell and just bought a new one.

As I used a rag dipped in turpentine to scrub the paint out of my hair, I swore that my jerry-rigging days were over. Never again would I crawl under the sink with a 10 lb plumbers wrench. No more making the sign of the cross as I turned off the electricity to replace light fixtures. I remember when my Dad had had enough, he would say, "Well, let's not be stupid and get killed in the process."

And, damn it, I was going to hire someone to sort out all of my financial gobbledy gook. Who knows how many financial opportunities I had lost due to my do-it-yourself financial planning. As I began working with financial professionals, I discovered that price is not the real issue. Rather, it is a combination of service, quality, and cost. The idea is not necessarily to get everything at low or no cost; instead, you want

You Don't Have to Be a Bag Lady!
A Humorous Survival Guide for the Reluctant Investor

to get what you pay for. Get the education you are paying for and have the relationship you want to receive for your money.

When it was time to do my taxes, I spread all my financial statements on the kitchen table. Tax laws change every year and I'm about as interested in keeping up with that as I am changing the oil in my car. I looked at the white/green refrigerator and scooped up all the papers. I said out loud to nobody, "Let's not be stupid and lose money in the process." I hired a professional. It would be cheaper in the long run.

Sheila Peters

Chapter 9
Giving Back

Can I really make a difference?

From birth to age 18, a girl needs good parents;
from 18 to 35 she needs good looks; from 35 to 55
she needs a good personality; and from 55 on she needs cash.
— Sophie Tucker

My first brush with philanthropy was in Sister Mary Faith's fourth grade class. Once a week, the mission box, a white can with a red cross, threaded and looped through the rows of desks. As we passed it along sheepishly, Sister smiled and nodded with each clink. I caught on quickly that five pennies turned more heads than a nickel. Sometimes, one of the rich kids from across North Avenue laboriously wedged a dollar bill through the slot, glancing up angelically for Sister's approval. On Sundays, we sealed quarters inside numbered envelopes and remorsefully dropped what could buy a whole lot of candy into the church basket. Judging by our dinner table conversations, *Fine. Send my plate to China—I hate peas,* I assumed the envelopes bought food for starving third world countries. Like my mother parking herself in a pew every Sunday "just in case it counts", I gave out of obligation or perhaps guilt. Hopefully, it would offset any minor infractions on Judgment Day. Of course, not the biggies on which I alone would have to pitch a defense.

But more than tithing, the best way for a Catholic to reach heaven was in performing acts of charity. We were all out of high school when my mother volunteered at church to make meals for a family in need. Once a week she cooked dinner for recovering Mrs. Foggarty, a 60-year-old woman who lived in a

Sheila Peters

bungalow three blocks away. Dinner usually consisted of a small meatloaf or one of Mom's mystery meat patties, some boiled-to-death vegetable and the family staple, cottage cheese, which was on our table 365 days of the year. I once told my mother that if the Queen of England was coming for dinner, cottage cheese would be part of that evening's fare.

Defensively she said, "Well, I imagine she'd like it."

Since feeding the poor was so rooted in my upbringing, as an adult I continued my mission by dishing out bologna sandwiches in shelters, slopping turkey and dressing onto plates in soup kitchens and schlepping bags of groceries in food pantries. If I could just keep the starving masses alive for one more day, I was doing my part.

Women and Volunteering

Throughout history, the role of volunteer and giver has been a traditional one for women. Women have shown their philanthropic spirit by establishing schools, founding hospitals and sheltering the homeless. Like most women, because I didn't have a lot of disposable income, I gave my time. And like most women, I never saw myself as a philanthropist, who in my mind was a prominent wealthy person. But oddly enough, even though women today are making more money, as a group they still don't give much of it away.

According to the Women's Philanthropy Institute, there are several reasons why women don't give money. Some women are so insecure about their finances, they are afraid to give. Even many women who have accumulated wealth are afraid of ending up as bag ladies. I must confess that when the stock market was benevolent, I reached for my checkbook. However, when my portfolio took a hit, you couldn't pry open my wallet with a crowbar.

Some women shrink from the responsibility and power associated with money. If they have traditionally been the peacekeepers in the family, they know money can stir things up and even divide families. If they do give, they would rather do so anonymously. Over the years, I made the mistake of giving small amounts to several organizations. My contribution couldn't have covered much more than the mailing expenses. I thought about giving anonymously to keep off mailing lists, but the wiser move would have been to give more money to one or two causes about which I felt strongly.

Some successful women don't give back to their male dominated schools or organizations because they didn't believe these institutions had helped them. Oftentimes they even held them back. Given these prevailing attitudes, it's no surprise that organizations haven't historically targeted women as serious philanthropists.

Inheriting Wealth

But, this is all changing. Women currently own more than half of the nation's investment wealth and will accumulate even more as their incomes increase. In addition, over 70 million baby boomers will be writing a large number of wills in the next decade and, unlike their parents, will have fewer children to pass their estates on to. Women will inherit much of the predicted $10 trillion intergenerational transfer of wealth in the coming decades. And because most women will be widowed or act as the principle wage earners, where that money goes will be primarily up to them. Much of it will go to the charities or organizations of their choice.

It is interesting to note that when women do give, they give very differently than men, who are more likely to support the arts and political organizations. Women need to feel connected with the cause and tend to donate to those related to health, the homeless, and the elderly.

Reinventing Fundraising by Sondra Shaw and Martha Taylor reports that "Women frequently give money to launch programs they view as bringing about social change. Men tend to give more out of organizational loyalty and support the status quo at their alma maters." This entrepreneurial desire to create may explain the growing popularity of women's funds over the past decade. These funds, which are supported by corporations and individual donors, award grants to organizations that help women fight obstacles they have had to endure such as domestic violence and financial inequality.

Local Funds

Recently, I had the opportunity to see the benefits of a local women's fund at work. The Bottomless Closet, a Chicago-based not-for-profit organization, gives low-income women business clothes for job interviews. The organization grew out of a radio program in which a young woman getting off welfare told of her frustration at not having appropriate interview clothing. A listener and her friends gathered all the business clothes they no longer wore and formed the Bottomless Closet. It became a place where low income job seekers can get two accessorized outfits right down to the shoes and handbags. After they land the job, they can have three more outfits.

When I dropped off clothes at the Bottomless Closet. I discovered that those in need aren't always low income and low education. I met a woman who had a good job as a college instructor until the day she ran away from an abusive husband with only the clothes on her back. Temporarily living in a women's shelter, she needed clothes with which to interview at the local college. The Bottomless Closet gave her two outfits and she landed the job on her first interview. Today, she volunteers at the Bottomless Closet helping to sort clothes, work with the clients and orchestrate programs. Beyond clothing, they need money to pay for office expenses and advertising. As it was, the office was staffed with only a single part time employee. The Bottomless Closet gets donations from individuals and local corporations but relies on women's foundations for the largest portion of their operating budgets.

One of the grant making foundations that supports them is The Chicago Foundation for Women. Since 1986, CFW has awarded 1424 grants totaling nearly $6 million to more than 500 organizations serving women and children. You can make a monetary donation directly to a local women's services organization of your choice or give it to a foundation, which in turn will award grants to various service organizations. To see a list of women's funds, refer to the Women's Fund Network at www.wfnet.org.

National Funds

There are currently more than 100 women's funds across the U.S., up from the eleven created in the 1970's. One of the more visible national funds, The Ms. Foundation for Women, (www.ms.foundation.org) was created 25 years ago and its founders included Gloria Steinem and Marlo Thomas. The Ms. Foundation supports economic development, domestic violence shelters, health services, reproductive choice, HIV/AIDS and many other issues.

Their national program, Take our Daughters to Work® Day, was developed to emphasize the importance of girls' abilities rather than appearance. A day at work helps girls make the connection between academic success and success in the real world. Seeing what women in particular do in the workplace helps girls make informed decisions about their futures. It's a chance to see their options.

International Funds

On the international front, the Global Fund for Women, www.globalfundforwomen.org was created in 1987 by three women who believed that the world changes from the ground up, one village at a time. They each put in $500. The foundation makes grants that support women's groups outside of the U.S. that are seeking not only increased resources, but greater power over their lives.

In 2000, the fund awarded over $3 million in grants to 333 women's groups in 95 countries. The fund helps women in Rwanda care for the thousands of children orphaned by the 1994 massacres. It pays the rent on a women's shelter in Bosnia. It gave $4,000 to a group of Mongolian women who traveled from village to village teaching women about ballots and parties so they could vote in the country's first democratic elections. The foundation discovered that the "empowerment" approach to economic and social development was central to any struggle, whether it be domestic violence or attaining credit. A quote on their website says it best: *Nobody can empower another person. Empowerment is not given, it is taken.*

At one time, each of these organizations was probably nothing more than a few women talking over coffee at someone's kitchen table. They started out small—in some cases with absolutely no money, but with a desire and commitment to improve women's lives. Whether you choose to give back in the form of money or time, your involvement can make a difference around the world or right in your own neighborhood.

If you would like to learn more about philanthropy, The Women's Philanthropy Institute in Madison, WI, (www.women-philanthropy.org) is an excellent educational resource. Martha Taylor of the WPI suggests eight strategies for effective giving.

1. Begin your philanthropy as early in life as possible. Even if you can't give as much as you'd like, your gifts will add up and begin to form your legacy.
2. Find your passion, and focus your gifts rather than scattering them. Think about two or three areas or causes you want to support and make this your

philanthropic mission. Not only will your gifts have more impact, but you will find your giving more satisfying.
3. Work for parity in giving in your household. You and your spouse should have equal say about which causes your contributions support and the amount given.
4. If you can, give out of principal to the causes you are passionate about. Think of your philanthropy as you would a child, your investment in the future of our world.
5. If you don't have much money, consider the strength of numbers. Organize with others to provide a pooled gift that can make a project possible.
6. Leverage your giving. Increase your impact by challenging others to support the causes you hold dear.
7. Teach the art of philanthropy to the next generation. Instill in your children, and the young people you associate with, the values you treasure and your commitment to support them.
8. Have fun with your philanthropy. Celebrate your birthday with a philanthropic gift that you might not have thought was possible. Surprise your friends by giving in their name-or to a nonprofit of their choice. The possibilities are endless!

If you hit the jackpot and are feeling generous with your loot, there is even a nonprofit organization that helps educate people of wealth on philanthropy. Refer to More Than Money (morethanmoney.org) to connect with organizations and causes that match your values.

***

Ignorance is what keeps women vulnerable. Empowerment, personal and financial, is the key that opens the door to choices

Sheila Peters

for women. Financial planning is a survival skill that should be honed long before a woman becomes widowed or divorced.

When I'm Mrs. Foggarty's age, I want to choose where to live and how to spend my time. If I plan ahead, hopefully my golden years won't be spent as a greeter at Walmart. I want to be a swinging blue-hair, filling my days with travel and other interests. God willing, I'll still be able to dink a tennis ball over the net without a walker. And because I want my friends there with me, I bug them constantly about their financial planning. After all, what good does it do me if all my friends end up as bag ladies?

You Don't Have to Be a Bag Lady!
A Humorous Survival Guide for the Reluctant Investor

Workbook

In 6 months you can have a better understanding of investing. You can also be on your way to having a solid financial plan of action. Dedicate one month to each task. You will be amazed how much you will learn and accomplish.

Month 1 - Assess Your Finances.

1. **Calculate your net worth**. (Assets minus liabilities). Subtract what you owe from what you own to determine your financial worth.

ASSETS

Cash

Cash/checking accounts	$_____
Savings	$_____
C/D and money markets	$_____
Cash value of life insurance policy	$_____

Fixed

Bonds and bond mutual funds	$_____
Treasury notes	$_____

Equity

Stocks	$_____
Mutual funds	$_____
Investment property	$_____
Businesses	$_____
Other	$_____
Total Liquid Assets	$_____

Sheila Peters

Personal
    Home $_____

    Automobiles $_____

    Jewelry $_____

    Other $_____

    Other $_____

    Total Personal Assets $_____

Retirement
    IRA $_____

    Employment savings plan $_____

    Pension $_____

    Other $_____

    Total Retirement Assets $_____

Total Assets
                                                      $_____

LIABILITIES

    Mortgage(s) $_____

    Credit cards $_____

    Bank loans $_____

    Auto loans $_____

    Other $_____

Total Liabilities
                                                      $_____

    Total Assets $_____

    Total Liabilities $_____

NET WORTH $_____

2. **Set your goals.** (long term and short term) You can't plan a strategy if you don't know where you want to end up. Put down all your goals, even the ones you think are just dreams. With planning, many of those dreams can become reality.

   Here are some sample goals:
   - Paying for college
   - Buying a car
   - Paying for a wedding
   - Buying a home
   - Second vacation home
   - Special travel
   - Saving for retirement
   - Retiring early
   - Starting your own business
   - Running away to Tahiti

   These are my immediate goals:

   - _____
   - _____

   These are my short-term goals to be achieved in 2-3 years:

   - _____
   - _____

   These are my long-term goals to be achieved in 5-10 years:

   - _____
   - _____

Sheila Peters

These are my plans for retirement:

- _____
- _____

You Don't Have to Be a Bag Lady!
A Humorous Survival Guide for the Reluctant Investor

3. **Determine your discretionary income.** (income minus expenses) Enter all of your incoming and outgoing money. Then you can decide how much you can afford to invest on a monthly basis. Be realistic because you want to stick with the amount you choose.

INCOME

Employment (net-after tax)	$_____
Self-employment	$_____
Social Security or govt benefits	$_____
Child support	$_____
Taxable investment income	$_____
Nontaxable investment income	$_____
Other	$_____
Other	$_____
Total Annual Income	$_____

EXPENSES (fixed)

Mortgage or rent	$_____
Real estate taxes	$_____
Homeowner's insurance	$_____
Condo fees etc.	$_____
Utilities	$_____
Food	$_____
Clothing	$_____
Personal care	$_____
Auto maintenance/insurance	$_____
Auto loan payment	$_____
Health insurance premiums	$_____
Other medical	$_____
Credit card payment	$_____

Sheila Peters

    Income tax payment $_____
    Life insurance $_____
    Tuition $_____
    Other $_____

    Total Fixed Expenses $_____

You Don't Have to Be a Bag Lady!
A Humorous Survival Guide for the Reluctant Investor

EXPENSES (discretionary)

Entertainment/dining	$_____
Recreation/travel	$_____
Charities	$_____
Gifts	$_____
Home improvement	$_____
Other	$_____
Other	$_____
Total Discretionary Expenses	$_____
Total All Expenses	$_____
TOTAL INCOME	$_____ (+)
TOTAL ALL EXPENSES	$_____ (-)
DISCRETIONARY INCOME (income minus expenses)	$_____

% You are willing to invest _____ %

(or) $_____

---

4. **Contact Social Security** (800/772-1213) Ask for Form SSA-7004 to request your earnings and benefits estimate statement. For all workers 25 years and older, Social Security will mail a benefits statement each year approximately 3 months before your birth month.

Month 2 - Watch, Read and Listen to Business News.

1. **Read** *The Wall Street Journal* at least once a week. Take note of the company names mentioned in the business section. Notice which companies and industries are hot.

2. **Listen to the business news** on the radio on your way to work. While making dinner, turn your TV to the business news.

3. **Watch** *Wall Street Week* on public television. Consult your TV directory for time and station or www.pbs.com. Jot down the names of companies they suggest. Are some companies mentioned repeatedly? Do any of them interest you enough to research?

Month 3 - Research Two Stocks Within the Same Industry.

1. **Read Value Line** for two companies that you like. The best comparisons will be within the same industry. Value Line is available at most libraries and is usually kept in large binders by the reference desk. Compare charts, stock prices, PE ratios, and the business summaries.

2. **Visit Web sites** www.morningstar.com and www.yahoo.com. Read the analysis on these same two stocks. Note how many brokers recommend to buy, sell or hold.

3. **Review the annual reports** for these two companies. Write to the companies for the reports or download them on the Internet. As you read, highlight important information such as recent performance and future outlook,

Month 4 - Research a Mutual Fund

1. **Visit Web sites of mutual fund companies** such as www.fidelity.com (800/544-8888) and www.vanguard.com (800/662-7447).

2. **Choose a fund** about which you would like to learn more.

3. **Request a prospectus** either by downloading or having a copy mailed. Highlight the important information.

4. **Research the fund** on www.morningstar.com. Look at the fund's performance for the past few years. Note what stocks they hold. What are the expenses? Is there a load?

Month 5 - Interview financial professionals.

1. **Attend free business seminars.** Look in your local newspaper for listings.

2. **If you would like to use a financial planner**, use one of the following:

   - The Institute of Certified Financial Planners, 1-800-282-7526 will provide background information on up to three planners in your area who are licensed as certified financial planners, plus information on how to pick a planner. You can also get information about selecting a planner on the ICFP's consumer education site, www.fp.edu/consumer/findFA.

   - The International Association for Financial Planning will provide a list of planners in your area plus information to help you choose a planner. Call 1-800-945-4237 or refer to their Web site, www.iaft.org.

- The National Association of Personal Financial Advisors, a trade group, will provide names of fee-only planners in your area who are paid by the client and do not receive commissions from investments they recommend. It also provides questions to ask a potential advisor. Call 1-888-862-4272. They also have a Web site, www.napfa.org.

- The Securities and Exchange Commission can tell you whether a financial planner is registered with the SEC as an investment advisor. The SEC also provides educational materials. Call 1-800-732-0330 or see their Web site at www.sec.gov.

Month 6 - Track your investments.

1. **Set up a free portfolio** on www.yahoo.com and track your two stocks. Observe price fluctuations. Use the Web sites to read recent news articles.

2. **Add more stocks to your portfolio** that you would like to track. To make it really interesting, plug in fictitious buys to see how your stocks would have fared.

3. **Track your actual investments** on www.yahoo.com.

Congratulations. You're on your way. Keep stretching yourself to learn more. Surround yourself with investors like yourself who are eager to learn. An investment club may give you the momentum you need to get going. Take one step at a time and be patient while your portfolio grows. Don't be swayed by the nay sayers who are waiting for the sky to fall. Be selective in what information you're willing to seriously consider. Remember, you're investing for the long term.

In time, you will discover that money can bestow the most important kind of power. The power to make your own choices. The power to lead the kind of life you want. Good luck and may you have a prosperous journey.

You Don't Have to Be a Bag Lady!
A Humorous Survival Guide for the Reluctant Investor

Resources

Mutual Fund Companies

Charles Schwab (800/5-NO-LOAD)   www.schwab.com
Fidelity   (800/544-8888)   www.fidelity.com
Janus Funds   (800/525-3713)   www.janus.com
Legg Mason Funds (800/822-5544) www.leggmason.com
Vanguard   (800/662-7447)   www.vanguard.com

(These are only a few; there are many more.)

Useful Web sites

Bloomberg   www.bloomberg.com
CBS Marketwatch   www.marketwatch.com
Cyberinvest   www.cyberinvest.com
Gomez Advisors   www.gomez.com
Investorguide   www.investorguide.com
Money Central   www.moneycentral.com
Morningstar   www.morningstar.net
Motley Fool   www.fool.com
MutualFund Education Alliance   www.mfea.com
Nightly Business Report   www.nbr.com
Quicken   www.quicken.com
Stock Detective   www.stockdetective.com
(exposes frauds & scams)
Stock Wizard   www.stockwizard.com
Yahoo   www.yahoo.com

Sheila Peters

Reports

Morningstar	Library Reference Desk
Standard & Poor's	Library Reference Desk
Value Line	Library Reference Desk

Additional Resources

Wall Street Week	www.pbs.org
Social Security Statements (800/772-1213)	www.ssa.gov

Works Cited

BOOKS

Brenner, Lynn, *Smart Questions to Ask Your Financial Advisers.* New York: Bloomberg Press, 1997.

Chesler, Phyllis, *Women and Madness.* New York: Doubleday and Co., 1972.

Chesler, Phyllis, *Women, Money and Power.* New York: William Morrow and Company, Inc., 1976.

Collins, Chuck and Rogers, Pam, *Robin Hood Was Right: A Guide to Giving Your Money for Social Change.* New York: W.W. Norton & Company, 2000

Dowling, Colette, *The Cinderella Complex.* New York: Simon & Schuster Inc, 1981.

Flores, Bettina and Sander, Jennifer Basye, *The Millionairess Across the Street.* Chicago, IL: Dearborn Financial Publishing, Inc., 1999.

Jaffe, Charles A., *The Right Way to Hire Financial Help.* Cambridge, MA: MIT Press, 1999.

Morris, Virginia B. and Morris, Kenneth M., *A Woman's Guide to Investing.* New York, NY: Lightbulb Press, 1999.

Peters, Tom, *The Circle of Innovation.* New York: Vintage Books, 1997.

Rowland, Mary, *A Common Sense Guide to Mutual Funds.* Princeton, NJ: Bloomberg Press, 1996.

Savage, Terry, *Terry Savage Talks Money: The Common-Sense Guide to Money Matters*. Chicago, IL: Dearborn Financial Pub., 1990.

Savage, Terry, *The Savage Truth on Money*. New York: John Wiley & Sons, Inc., 1999.

Shaw, Sondra C. and Taylor, Martha A., *Reinventing Fundraising: Realizing the Potential of Women's Philanthropy*. San Francisco, CA: Jossey-Bass Inc., Publishers, 1995.

Stanley, Thomas and Danko, William, *The Millionaire Next Door*. Marietta, GA: Longstreet Press, Inc., 1996.

Stanny, Barbara, *Prince Charming Isn't Coming: How Women Get Smart About Money*. New York: Penguin Putnam Inc., 1997.

Tyson, Eric, *Investing For Dummies*. Foster City, CA: IDG Books Worldwide, Inc., 1996.

Tyson, Eric, *Mutual Funds For Dummies*. Foster City, CA: IDG Books Worldwide, Inc., 1998.

Wuorio, Jeff, *Got Money? Enjoy it! Manage it! Even Save Some of it!* New York: AMA Publications, 1999.

About the Author

Sheila Peters, a Chicago native, is an active investor and member of the National Association of Investors Corporation (NAIC), Chicago West Chapter. She is passionate about women empowering themselves by learning about and investing in the stock market. She also participates in a women's investment club. She has a M.S. in Written Communications and has been published in the *Chicago Tribune* and various magazines.